From Dugout to Devotion- Spiritual Lessons from Baseball

Joshua Rhoades

Published by Joshua Paul Rhoades, 2024.

While every precaution has been taken in the preparation of this book, the publisher assumes no responsibility for errors or omissions, or for damages resulting from the use of the information contained herein.

FROM DUGOUT TO DEVOTION- SPIRITUAL LESSONS FROM BASEBALL

First edition. August 26, 2024.

Copyright © 2024 Joshua Rhoades.

ISBN: 979-8227653376

Written by Joshua Rhoades.

Also by Joshua Rhoades

Courage Under Fire: David's Stand On The Battlefield
Jonah's Journey: Voices Of Redemption And Lessons In Obedience
The Furnace Of Faith: 12 Principles From The Heat Of Faith
Whispers of Hope: Inspiring Stories of Men's Prayers In Scripture
Frontier Legends: The Oregon Dream
Elijah: A Beacon Of Boldness
HOOK, LINE & SAVIOUR - Faith Reflections from Fishing
Driven By Faith: Motor Racing Inspired Christian Life
30 Day Devotional - Bold and Strong- Coffee Devotions for a
Courageous Christian Walk
Authentic Christianity: The Heart of Old Time Religion
Consider The Ant - God's Tiny Preachers
Flee Fornication: The Plea For Purity
Renewed Hope- How to Find Encouragement in God
Sounding The Call - The Voice of Conviction
The Altar - Where Heaven Meets Earth
The Bible's Battlefields- Timeless Lessons from Ancient Wars
The Sacred Art of Silence - How Silence Speaks in Scripture
Under Fire- The Sanctity of the Traditional Biblical Home
Who Is on the Lord's Side? A Call to Righteousness
What Is Truth? - From Skepticism to Submission
From Dugout to Devotion- Spiritual Lessons from Baseball
The Immutable Fortress- Security in God's Unchanging Nature

Chapter 1 - Develop Fundamental Skills

"Therefore leaving the principles of the doctrine of Christ, let us go on unto perfection; not laying again the foundation of repentance from dead works, and of faith toward God." Hebrews 6:1"

To become a successful baseball player, it's essential to develop fundamental skills, which are the building blocks of the game. Mastering the basic skills of hitting, fielding, throwing, and running is crucial. Hitting involves timing, hand-eye coordination, and understanding how to read pitches. Practice swinging the bat, focus on making solid contact with the ball, and learn to hit in different situations. Fielding requires agility, quick reflexes, and precise coordination to catch ground balls, fly balls, and line drives. Practice fielding drills, work on your footwork, and develop a quick and accurate throw. Throwing is about having a strong and accurate arm, knowing the proper throwing mechanics, and being able to throw from different positions and angles. Regularly practice throwing drills, aim for consistent accuracy, and strengthen your arm through specific exercises. Running, an often overlooked skill, is essential for base running, stealing bases, and defensive plays. Focus on improving your speed, learn proper running techniques, and practice running the bases efficiently. By honing these basic skills, a baseball player can become more confident, versatile, and effective on the field.

In the life of a Christian, developing fundamental skills parallels mastering the basic principles of faith, such as love, faith, and prayer. Just as in baseball, these fundamentals form the foundation of a strong spiritual life. Love is at the core of Christian teachings. It involves showing kindness, compassion, and understanding to others. Practicing love means following the example of Jesus by caring for others, forgiving those who have wronged us, and putting others' needs before our own. Faith is the belief and trust in God. It's about having confidence in God's plan and His promises. Strengthening your faith involves reading the Bible, participating in worship, and surrounding yourself with a supportive community of believers. Prayer is the way Christians communicate with God. It involves praising God, asking for guidance, confessing sins, and interceding for others. Developing a consistent prayer life means setting aside regular time for prayer, being honest with God about your thoughts and feelings, and listening for His guidance. By mastering these basic principles of the faith, a Christian can grow spiritually, build a strong relationship with God, and live a life that reflects God's love and grace.

The Bible verse Hebrews 6:1 says, "Therefore leaving the principles of the doctrine of Christ, let us go on unto perfection; not laying again the foundation of repentance from dead works, and of faith toward God." This verse emphasizes the importance of moving beyond the basics and striving for spiritual maturity. It encourages Christians to build upon their foundational principles and continue growing in their faith. Just as a baseball player must continuously improve and refine their skills, a Christian must strive to deepen their understanding of God and grow in their spiritual journey.

In both baseball and the Christian life, mastering the fundamentals is just the beginning. For a baseball player, once the basic skills are developed, it's important to continuously practice and refine them. This involves regular training, seeking feedback from coaches, and being open to learning new techniques. Similarly, for a Christian, mastering the basic principles of faith involves ongoing spiritual growth. This includes studying the Bible, participating in church activities, seeking guidance from spiritual mentors, and being open to the Holy Spirit's work in your life.

The journey to perfection, both in baseball and in faith, requires dedication, perseverance, and a willingness to grow. A successful baseball player is always looking for ways to improve, whether it's through practicing more, studying the game, or learning from others. Similarly, a growing Christian is always seeking to deepen their relationship with God, whether it's through prayer, Bible study, or serving others. Both require a commitment to continuous improvement and a desire to achieve excellence.

In conclusion, developing fundamental skills in baseball is essential for success on the field, just as mastering the basic principles of faith is crucial for a strong and growing Christian life. Both require dedication, practice, and a commitment to continuous improvement. By focusing on the basics and striving for growth, a baseball player can become more skilled and confident, and a Christian can deepen their relationship with God and live a life that reflects His love and grace. The journey to perfection, whether in baseball or in faith, is a lifelong process that involves perseverance, dedication, and a willingness to grow and learn. By staying committed to mastering the fundamentals, both baseball players and Christians can achieve their goals and live fulfilling lives.

Chapter 2 - Practice Regularly

"Pray without ceasing." 1 Thessalonians 5:17

Consistent practice is essential for improving your skills and maintaining your fitness as a baseball player. This means dedicating time each day to practice your hitting, fielding, throwing, and running. Consistent practice helps you to build muscle memory, which makes your movements more natural and automatic. When you practice regularly, you also develop your strength and endurance, which are crucial for performing at your best during games. For example, practicing your swing every day helps you to refine your technique and timing, making it easier to hit the ball accurately and with power. Similarly, regularly practicing your fielding skills helps you to react quickly and make precise plays. Throwing practice is essential for developing arm strength and accuracy, while running drills help you to improve your speed and agility on the bases. In addition to skill practice, maintaining your overall fitness through regular exercise and conditioning is important. This can include strength training, cardiovascular workouts, and flexibility exercises. By committing to regular practice and fitness routines, you will be better prepared for the physical demands of baseball and more likely to perform well under pressure.

In the life of a Christian, regularly practicing spiritual disciplines is equally important for maintaining and growing your faith. Just as consistent practice is essential for a baseball player, spiritual disciplines like prayer, reading the Bible, and worship should be practiced regularly to strengthen your relationship with God. Prayer is a vital part of the Christian life, providing a way to communicate with God, express gratitude, seek guidance, and intercede for others. The Bible verse 1 Thessalonians 5:17 says, "Pray without ceasing," emphasizing the importance of maintaining a continual conversation with God throughout your day. This doesn't mean you need to be on your knees in prayer all day, but rather that you should have a mindset of openness and ongoing dialogue with God, bringing your thoughts, concerns, and praises to Him regularly.

Reading the Bible is another essential spiritual discipline. The Bible is God's Word and provides guidance, wisdom, and encouragement. Regularly reading and studying the Bible helps you to understand God's character, His promises, and His will for your life. It also equips you with the knowledge and truth needed to navigate life's challenges and make decisions that honor God. By immersing yourself in scripture, you can grow in your faith and be better prepared to share it with others.

Worship is a vital part of the Christian life as well. Worshiping God through song, prayer, and other acts of reverence helps to keep your focus on Him and reminds you of His greatness and goodness. Worship can take place both individually and corporately, such as in a church setting. Corporate worship provides an opportunity to gather with other believers, offering mutual encouragement and support, while individual worship allows for personal reflection and intimacy with God.

Regularly practicing these spiritual disciplines—prayer, reading the Bible, and worship—helps to build a strong foundation for your faith. Just as a baseball player improves with regular practice, a Christian grows in their faith and spiritual maturity by consistently engaging in these disciplines. This regular practice helps to keep your faith active and vibrant, allowing you to experience a deeper relationship with God and a greater sense of His presence in your life.

In addition to these primary disciplines, other spiritual practices such as fasting, journaling, and acts of service can also contribute to spiritual growth. Fasting, for example, is a way to seek God's guidance and draw closer to Him by temporarily giving up something important, such as food. Journaling can help you to reflect on your spiritual journey, record answered prayers, and document lessons learned. Acts of service demonstrate God's love to others and provide opportunities to live out your faith in practical ways.

Regularly practicing these disciplines also helps to build spiritual resilience. Just as a baseball player becomes more confident and capable through consistent practice, a Christian becomes more steadfast in their faith through regular spiritual practice. This resilience is crucial for facing the challenges and trials of life with faith and courage. It helps to keep you grounded in God's truth and promises, even when circumstances are difficult or uncertain.

Moreover, regular practice fosters spiritual growth and transformation. As you consistently engage in prayer, scripture reading, and worship, you are continually being shaped and molded by God's Word and His Spirit. This ongoing transformation helps you to become more like Christ in your thoughts, attitudes, and actions. It enables you to live out your faith more fully and effectively, impacting those around you with God's love and grace.

In conclusion, consistent practice is essential for improving your skills and maintaining your fitness as a baseball player, just as regularly practicing spiritual disciplines is crucial for growing in faith and maintaining a strong relationship with God. Both require dedication, commitment, and a willingness to invest time and effort. By practicing regularly, whether in baseball or in your spiritual life, you can develop the skills and resilience needed to succeed and thrive. The discipline of regular practice helps to build a strong foundation, fosters growth and transformation, and prepares you to face challenges with confidence and faith. By committing to regular practice, you can achieve your goals and live a fulfilling and meaningful life, both on the baseball field and in your walk with God.

Chapter 3 - Join a Team

"Not forsaking the assembling of ourselves together, as the manner of some is; but exhorting one another: and so much the more, as ye see the day approaching." Hebrews 10:25

Joining a team is a crucial step for any aspiring baseball player because participating in organized baseball allows you to gain valuable experience and learn the importance of teamwork. When you join a team, you have the opportunity to play alongside others who share your passion for the game, which can be both inspiring and motivating. Being part of a team teaches you how to collaborate with others, understand different roles and responsibilities, and work together toward a common goal. In baseball, every player has a specific role, whether it's pitching, catching, fielding, or hitting, and the success of the team depends on how well each player performs their role and supports their teammates. By participating in team practices, games, and other activities, you learn to communicate effectively, trust your teammates, and develop a sense of camaraderie. This teamwork is essential for winning games and achieving success on the field, as it fosters a supportive environment where players can rely on each other and work together to overcome challenges. Additionally, playing on a team provides structured opportunities to practice and improve your skills under the guidance of coaches who can offer valuable feedback and instruction. Coaches help players to refine their techniques, understand game strategies, and develop a deeper knowledge of baseball. Being part of a team also allows you to experience the excitement and intensity of competition, which can drive you to push your limits and strive for excellence. The friendships and bonds formed within a team can last a lifetime, creating a network of support both on and off the field.

In the life of a Christian, being part of a church community is equally important for growing in faith and fellowship. Just as joining a baseball team helps you to develop your skills and learn the value of teamwork, being active in a church community helps you to grow spiritually and build strong relationships with other believers. The Bible verse Hebrews 10:25 says, "Not forsaking the assembling of ourselves together, as the manner of some is; but exhorting one another: and so much the more, as ye see the day approaching." This verse emphasizes the importance of gathering together with other believers to encourage and support each other in the faith. By regularly attending church services, Bible studies, and other church activities, you can deepen your understanding of God's Word, receive spiritual encouragement, and find guidance and support from fellow Christians. Being part of a church community provides opportunities for worship, where you can collectively praise and honor God, and for fellowship, where you can build meaningful relationships with others who share your faith. These relationships can provide a source of strength and encouragement, especially during difficult times, as you can rely on your church family for prayer, support, and practical help. Just as a baseball team works together to achieve common goals, a church community works together to grow in faith, serve others, and spread the message of the gospel. Engaging in church activities, such as volunteering for service projects, participating in small groups, or joining ministry teams, allows you to use your gifts and talents to contribute to the life of the church and make a positive impact on others. Through these experiences, you can develop a sense of belonging and purpose, knowing that you are part of something greater than yourself.

Being part of a church community also provides accountability, as fellow believers can help you stay committed to your faith and encourage you to live according to God's principles. Just as teammates hold each other accountable on the baseball field, church members can hold each other accountable in their spiritual walk, offering encouragement, correction, and support when needed. This accountability helps you to stay focused on your spiritual goals and grow in your relationship with God. Moreover, being involved in a church community allows you to learn from others who have more experience and wisdom in the faith. Just as a baseball player can learn from more experienced teammates and coaches, Christians can learn from pastors, elders, and mature believers who can provide guidance, mentorship, and inspiration. These relationships can help you to deepen your understanding of the Bible, grow in your faith, and navigate the challenges of life with a biblical perspective.

In addition to the spiritual growth and support that a church community provides, it also offers opportunities for outreach and evangelism. Just as a baseball team represents their school or community in competitions, the church represents Christ to the world. By participating in outreach activities, mission trips, and evangelistic events, you can share the love of Christ with others and make a difference in your community and beyond. These experiences not only help to spread the gospel but also strengthen your own faith as you see God at work in the lives of others. Being part of a church community allows you to be part of a collective effort to fulfill the Great Commission, making disciples of all nations and bringing glory to God.

In conclusion, joining a team is essential for any baseball player to gain experience, learn teamwork, and develop skills, just as being part of a church community is crucial for a Christian to grow in faith, receive support, and build meaningful relationships. Both require commitment, participation, and a willingness to work together with others toward common goals. By being part of a team, whether on the baseball field or in the church, you can experience the joy of camaraderie, the satisfaction of achieving shared goals, and the growth that comes from learning and supporting one another. The principles of teamwork, commitment, and mutual support are key to success in both baseball and the Christian life. Through regular participation and engagement in these communities, you can develop your skills, deepen your faith, and make a positive impact on those around you.

Chapter 4 - Study the Game

"Study to shew thyself approved unto God, a workman that needeth not to be ashamed, rightly dividing the word of truth." 2 Timothy 2:15

To become a successful baseball player, it's essential to study the game and understand its rules, strategies, and nuances. Baseball is a complex sport with a rich history and intricate details that go beyond simply hitting the ball and running bases. Understanding the rules of baseball is fundamental. This includes knowing the basic rules of play, such as how runs are scored, how outs are made, and the different roles of each player on the field. It also involves understanding more specific rules, like those governing balks, infield fly rules, and how to properly appeal plays. Mastering the rules allows you to play the game correctly and make strategic decisions during play. Additionally, understanding the strategies involved in baseball is crucial. This includes knowing when to bunt, steal a base, or employ a hit-and-run play. Strategies can vary based on the situation in the game, the strengths and weaknesses of your team, and the tendencies of your opponents. Knowing how to read the game and make smart decisions can give your team a competitive edge. For example, understanding how pitchers work can help you anticipate pitches and improve your hitting. Recognizing defensive alignments can guide you in making smarter base-running decisions. Studying the game also means appreciating its nuances, such as the psychological aspects of competition and the importance of teamwork and communication. Baseball is a mental game as much as it is a physical one, and being able to stay focused, handle pressure, and maintain a positive attitude are key components of success. Watching professional games, analyzing plays, and learning from experienced players and coaches can deepen your understanding of these nuances and enhance your overall performance.

In the life of a Christian, studying the Bible is just as important for understanding God's commandments and His will for your life. The Bible is the foundational text for Christians, providing guidance, wisdom, and insight into living a life that honors God. The Bible verse 2 Timothy 2:15 says, "Study to shew thyself approved unto God, a workman that needeth not to be ashamed, rightly dividing the word of truth." This verse emphasizes the importance of diligent study and accurate understanding of God's Word. Studying the Bible helps Christians understand God's commandments, His promises, and His character. It reveals the story of God's relationship with humanity, from creation to the promise of eternal life through Jesus Christ. By studying the Bible, Christians learn about the principles and values that should guide their lives, such as love, justice, mercy, and humility. It also helps them to discern God's will and make decisions that align with His purposes.

Regular Bible study can take many forms, including personal reading, group studies, and listening to sermons and teachings. Personal Bible study allows you to spend time reflecting on God's Word and how it applies to your life. Group studies provide the opportunity to discuss and explore the scriptures with others, gaining different perspectives and insights. Listening to sermons and teachings from knowledgeable pastors and teachers can deepen your understanding and provide practical applications for daily living. Just as understanding baseball's rules and strategies helps you play better, understanding the Bible helps you live a more faithful and effective Christian life.

Moreover, studying the Bible equips Christians to share their faith with others. Just as a knowledgeable baseball player can explain the game to someone new, a well-studied Christian can share the gospel and answer questions about their faith with confidence and clarity. This is important for fulfilling the Great Commission, which calls Christians to make disciples of all nations. Studying the Bible also helps Christians grow in their relationship with God. Through reading and meditating on scripture, they come to know God more deeply and understand His love and grace. This relationship is the foundation of the Christian life, providing strength, comfort, and direction.

The Bible also offers practical guidance for everyday living. It addresses issues such as relationships, work, ethics, and personal conduct. By applying biblical principles to these areas, Christians can navigate life's challenges with wisdom and integrity. Just as a baseball player uses their knowledge of the game to make strategic decisions, Christians use their knowledge of the Bible to make choices that reflect their faith and honor God. Additionally, the Bible provides examples of faithful living through the stories of biblical characters. By studying these stories, Christians can learn from the successes and failures of others and find inspiration for their own spiritual journey.

The discipline of studying the Bible requires commitment and consistency, much like the discipline of studying the game of baseball. It involves setting aside regular time for reading and reflection, seeking to understand the context and meaning of the scriptures, and being open to the Holy Spirit's guidance. Just as a baseball player might review game footage to improve, a Christian might revisit certain passages or themes in the Bible to deepen their understanding and application.

In conclusion, studying the game of baseball is essential for understanding its rules, strategies, and nuances, just as studying the Bible is crucial for understanding God's commandments and His will for your life. Both require dedication, effort, and a desire to learn and grow. By studying the game, a baseball player can improve their performance and contribute to their team's success. By studying the Bible, a Christian can grow in faith, live according to God's principles, and positively impact others. The principles of diligent study, continuous learning, and practical application are key to success in both baseball and the Christian life. Through committed study and reflection, both baseball players and Christians can achieve their goals and live fulfilling lives.

Chapter 5 - Physical Fitness

"Know ye not that your body is the temple of the Holy Ghost which is in you, which ye have of God, and ye are not your own?" 1 Corinthians 6:19

Maintaining a high level of physical fitness is essential for any aspiring baseball player, and this can be achieved through a combination of strength training, agility exercises, and endurance workouts. Physical fitness is the foundation of athletic performance, and in baseball, it plays a crucial role in all aspects of the game, from hitting and pitching to fielding and base running. Strength training helps to build muscle, increase power, and improve overall body composition. Exercises such as weightlifting, resistance training, and bodyweight exercises like push-ups and squats are key components of a strength training regimen. These exercises not only enhance muscular strength but also contribute to better coordination and stability, which are vital for executing powerful swings and strong throws. Agility exercises, on the other hand, focus on improving speed, quickness, and the ability to change direction rapidly. Drills such as ladder drills, cone drills, and shuttle runs help to develop agility, enabling players to react swiftly on the field, whether it's chasing down a fly ball or stealing a base. Endurance workouts are equally important as they enhance cardiovascular health and stamina, allowing players to maintain high levels of performance throughout the game. Activities such as running, cycling, and interval training improve endurance, ensuring that players can sustain their energy and focus during long games and intense practices.

In the life of a Christian, maintaining physical fitness is paralleled by the biblical principle of keeping your body, the temple of the Holy Spirit, healthy and strong. The Bible verse 1 Corinthians 6:19 states, "Know ye not that your body is the temple of the Holy Ghost which is in you, which ye have of God, and ye are not your own?" This verse underscores the importance of treating our bodies with respect and care because they are dwelling places of the Holy Spirit. Just as a baseball player prioritizes physical fitness to enhance their athletic abilities, Christians are called to maintain their physical health to honor God and fulfill their spiritual responsibilities.

Taking care of one's body involves making healthy lifestyle choices such as eating a balanced diet, getting adequate rest, and avoiding harmful substances. Proper nutrition fuels the body, providing the necessary vitamins, minerals, and energy to perform both physically and mentally. A balanced diet rich in fruits, vegetables, lean proteins, and whole grains supports overall health and well-being. Hydration is also crucial, as staying hydrated helps to regulate body temperature, keep joints lubricated, and transport nutrients throughout the body. Rest and recovery are vital components of physical fitness. Ensuring adequate sleep allows the body to repair and rebuild, leading to improved performance and reduced risk of injury.

Similarly, spiritual fitness involves regular practices that strengthen one's faith and relationship with God. These practices include prayer, reading the Bible, worship, and fellowship with other believers. Just as physical exercises build muscle and endurance, spiritual disciplines build spiritual strength and resilience. Prayer is a way to communicate with God, seeking His guidance and expressing gratitude. Regular Bible study deepens understanding of God's Word and helps apply biblical principles to daily life. Worship, whether in a communal setting or individually, allows believers to express their love and reverence for God. Fellowship with other Christians provides support, encouragement, and accountability, helping individuals to stay committed to their faith.

Avoiding harmful behaviors and substances is as important in spiritual fitness as it is in physical fitness. Just as a baseball player avoids drugs and unhealthy habits to maintain peak performance, Christians are called to avoid sin and behaviors that can harm their spiritual health.

This includes staying away from situations that can lead to temptation and making choices that align with biblical values. Regular self-examination and repentance help to keep one's spiritual life pure and focused on God.

Physical fitness also plays a role in serving others and fulfilling God's work. A healthy and strong body enables Christians to engage in various forms of ministry and service, whether it's helping those in need, participating in mission trips, or being active in church activities. Good physical health allows individuals to have the energy and vitality needed to serve effectively and make a positive impact in their communities.

Moreover, maintaining physical fitness can be a form of worship and gratitude to God. By taking care of the body that God has given, Christians can show appreciation for His creation and demonstrate a commitment to living a life that honors Him. Physical activities can also be opportunities for fellowship and outreach, such as participating in church sports leagues or community fitness programs.

In conclusion, maintaining a high level of physical fitness through strength training, agility exercises, and endurance workouts is crucial for success in baseball, just as keeping your body healthy and strong is vital for a fruitful Christian life. Both require dedication, discipline, and a commitment to making healthy choices. By prioritizing physical fitness, baseball players can enhance their performance and longevity in the sport. Similarly, by treating the body as a temple of the Holy Spirit, Christians can honor God, improve their overall well-being, and be better equipped to serve others. The principles of regular exercise, healthy living, and spiritual discipline are interconnected, contributing to a holistic approach to health and faith. Whether on the field or in daily life, maintaining physical and spiritual fitness leads to a more fulfilling and impactful existence. Through consistent effort and a focus on holistic health, individuals can achieve their goals, honor God, and make a positive difference in the world around them.

Chapter 6 - Mental Toughness

"Thou therefore endure hardness, as a good soldier of Jesus Christ." 2 Timothy 2:3

Developing mental toughness is crucial for any aspiring baseball player, as it enables them to handle the pressures of competition and perform at their best, even in challenging situations. Mental toughness is the ability to stay focused, remain positive, and bounce back from setbacks, which are all essential qualities for success in baseball. The game can be mentally demanding, with the constant pressure to perform, the possibility of making errors, and the need to stay calm under pressure. Building mental resilience involves practicing techniques such as visualization, where you imagine yourself successfully executing plays, which can help boost confidence and reduce anxiety. Positive self-talk is another important technique, where you encourage yourself with affirmations and constructive thoughts, helping to keep negative emotions at bay. Developing a pre-game routine can also help you mentally prepare for competition by establishing a sense of control and focus. Regularly facing and overcoming difficult situations in practice, such as high-pressure drills or competitive scrimmages, can also build mental toughness, making it easier to handle similar pressures during actual games. Learning to stay present and focused on the current moment, rather than dwelling on past mistakes or worrying about future outcomes, is crucial for maintaining peak performance. Just as physical training strengthens the body, mental training strengthens the mind, helping you to remain composed and perform consistently, even under stress.

In the life of a Christian, developing spiritual resilience is equally important for handling life's challenges and staying faithful. Spiritual resilience is the ability to maintain faith and trust in God, even when facing hardships, uncertainties, and trials. The Bible verse 2 Timothy 2:3 says, "Thou therefore endure hardness, as a good soldier of Jesus Christ." This verse highlights the importance of enduring difficulties with strength and perseverance, drawing a parallel between the discipline of a soldier and the steadfastness required in the Christian faith. Just as a soldier must be mentally prepared to face battles, Christians must be spiritually prepared to face the challenges of life.

Building spiritual resilience involves regular practices that strengthen your faith and deepen your relationship with God. Prayer is a vital part of this process, providing a way to seek God's guidance, express your concerns, and find comfort in His presence. Through prayer, you can cultivate a sense of peace and trust, knowing that God is in control and has a purpose for every situation. Reading and meditating on the Bible is another key practice, as scripture offers wisdom, encouragement, and reminders of God's promises. By immersing yourself in God's Word, you can gain perspective on your circumstances and find the strength to persevere. Fellowship with other believers is also crucial for building spiritual resilience. Being part of a supportive community provides encouragement, accountability, and the opportunity to share burdens and victories with others. Through mutual support and prayer, you can draw strength from the collective faith and experiences of fellow Christians. Engaging in regular worship, whether individually or corporately, helps to keep your focus on God and reminds you of His greatness and faithfulness.

Facing and overcoming challenges is a natural part of building resilience, both mentally and spiritually. Just as a baseball player grows stronger by pushing through difficult practices and games, Christians grow stronger by relying on God through trials and tribulations. Each challenge is an opportunity to trust God more deeply and to witness His faithfulness in action. This process of overcoming difficulties and seeing God's provision builds a foundation of faith that can withstand future storms. Maintaining a positive mindset is essential for both mental and spiritual resilience. In baseball, staying positive helps players to recover quickly from mistakes and stay focused on the next play. Similarly, in the Christian life, maintaining a hopeful outlook and trusting in God's goodness helps to navigate difficult times without becoming overwhelmed by negativity or despair. Positive thinking, grounded in faith, can transform how you perceive and respond to challenges.

Setting goals and staying motivated is another important aspect of resilience. In baseball, setting performance goals can keep you focused and driven, while in the Christian life, setting spiritual goals can help you stay committed to growing in your faith. Whether it's committing to daily prayer, reading the Bible, or serving others, having clear objectives provides direction and purpose.

Adapting to change is also a key component of resilience. Baseball players must adapt to changing game situations, different opponents, and varying conditions, just as Christians must adapt to life's ever-changing circumstances. Flexibility and the ability to adjust your approach based on the situation are important for maintaining resilience and effectiveness.

In both baseball and the Christian life, resilience is built through consistent practice, perseverance, and a reliance on foundational principles. Just as mental toughness in baseball is developed through rigorous training and a positive mindset, spiritual resilience is developed through regular spiritual practices and a deep trust in God. By cultivating resilience, you can navigate the pressures and challenges of life with confidence and faith, knowing that you are equipped to handle whatever comes your way.

In conclusion, developing mental toughness is essential for handling the pressures of competition in baseball, just as developing spiritual resilience is crucial for navigating life's challenges and staying faithful as a Christian. Both require a commitment to regular practice, a positive mindset, and the ability to adapt and persevere. By building mental and spiritual resilience, you can achieve success and fulfillment in both your athletic and spiritual pursuits. The principles of focus, perseverance, and trust in foundational truths are key to developing resilience, helping you to face challenges with strength and confidence. Whether on the baseball field or in your spiritual journey, resilience equips you to overcome obstacles and emerge stronger, more capable, and more faithful.

Chapter 7 - Work on Batting Technique

"And whatsoever ye do, do it heartily, as to the Lord, and not unto men." Colossians 3:23

To become a successful baseball player, it is crucial to work on your batting technique by focusing on your batting stance, swing mechanics, and hand-eye coordination. The batting stance is the foundation of a good hit; it involves positioning your feet properly, maintaining a balanced posture, and being ready to swing. Your stance should be comfortable and allow for a smooth, powerful swing. Swing mechanics are equally important. This includes the proper grip on the bat, the motion of your arms, the rotation of your hips, and the follow-through. Each part of the swing must be coordinated to ensure maximum power and accuracy. Regularly practicing your swing, with attention to these details, can greatly improve your hitting performance. Hand-eye coordination is also essential for making contact with the ball. Drills that focus on tracking the ball with your eyes and reacting quickly can help enhance this skill. Techniques such as using a batting tee, soft toss, and live pitching are effective ways to practice and refine your batting skills. Consistent practice, feedback from coaches, and a focus on technique can lead to significant improvements in your ability to hit the ball effectively.

In the life of a Christian, focusing on spiritual practices with proper understanding and dedication is just as important. Spiritual practices, such as prayer, reading the Bible, worship, and service, form the foundation of a strong and growing faith. Just as a baseball player must pay attention to their batting technique, Christians must approach their spiritual practices with intentionality and commitment. The Bible verse Colossians 3:23 says, "And whatsoever ye do, do it heartily, as to the Lord, and not unto men." This verse emphasizes the importance of dedicating our efforts to God, doing everything with sincerity and devotion. Prayer is a fundamental spiritual practice that involves communicating with God. It is a way to express gratitude, seek guidance, confess sins, and intercede for others. Effective prayer requires sincerity and a heart that seeks to connect with God. Developing a consistent prayer routine, setting aside specific times each day for prayer, and creating a quiet space can enhance the quality of your prayer life. Just as a batter focuses on their stance and swing, Christians should focus on approaching prayer with reverence and attentiveness.

Reading the Bible is another essential practice. The Bible provides guidance, wisdom, and insight into God's will and character. Regular Bible study helps Christians understand God's commandments and apply His teachings to their daily lives. It involves not just reading the words, but meditating on them, seeking to understand their deeper meaning, and how they apply to personal circumstances. Like a batter who practices their swing repeatedly, Christians should consistently engage with the Bible to deepen their understanding and strengthen their faith. Worship is also a crucial aspect of the Christian life. Worship can take place in a communal setting, such as church services, or individually through personal expressions of praise and devotion. Worshiping God involves recognizing His greatness, expressing gratitude, and surrendering to His will. It helps to keep our focus on God and reminds us of His love and faithfulness. Just as a baseball player needs to practice and refine their technique, Christians need to regularly engage in worship to maintain a close relationship with God.

Service to others is another important spiritual practice. Serving others in love reflects the heart of Christ and fulfills His command to love our neighbors. This can involve volunteering, helping those in need, and using our gifts and talents to benefit others. Service requires dedication and a willingness to put others' needs before our own, much like the discipline required to master a batting technique. By serving others, Christians live out their faith in practical ways, demonstrating the love of God through their actions. In conclusion, working on batting technique involves focusing on your batting stance, swing mechanics, and hand-eye coordination, just as focusing on spiritual practices with proper understanding and dedication is essential for a strong Christian life. Both require intentionality, consistency, and a commitment to improvement. By dedicating time and effort to refine these skills, whether in baseball or in your spiritual journey, you can achieve greater success and fulfillment. The principles of dedication, practice, and heartfelt commitment are key to excelling in both areas, helping you to grow and thrive in your pursuits.

Chapter 8 - Improve Pitching Skills

"But sanctify the Lord God in your hearts: and be ready always to give an answer to every man that asketh you a reason of the hope that is in you with meekness and fear."

1 Peter 3:15

To become a successful baseball pitcher, it's essential to improve your pitching skills by focusing on your pitching mechanics, control, and velocity. Pitching mechanics are the foundational techniques that allow you to throw accurately and powerfully without injuring yourself. This involves understanding the proper way to position your body, how to grip the baseball, and how to execute your delivery smoothly and consistently. A good pitcher practices their windup, stride, and follow-through repeatedly to ensure that each pitch is thrown with precision and efficiency. Control, or the ability to throw strikes and place the ball exactly where you want it, is crucial for keeping batters off balance and reducing the number of walks. This can be improved by working on your release point, refining your grip, and consistently practicing your pitches. Different pitches, such as fastballs, curveballs, and sliders, require different grips and techniques, so mastering these is essential for a versatile pitcher. Velocity, or the speed at which you throw the ball, can make your pitches more difficult for batters to hit. Improving velocity often involves strength training, particularly focusing on your core and lower body, as well as exercises that increase arm speed and overall athleticism. Working with a pitching coach can provide valuable feedback and guidance, helping you to identify areas for improvement and develop a tailored training plan. Consistent practice, combined with a focus on mechanics, control, and velocity, can transform a good pitcher into a great one, making you a vital asset to your team.

In the life of a Christian, developing the ability to share and defend your faith with clarity and confidence is equally important. Just as a pitcher works on their mechanics, control, and velocity, Christians must work on their understanding of the faith, their ability to communicate it effectively, and their confidence in sharing it. The Bible verse 1 Peter 3:15 says, "But sanctify the Lord God in your hearts: and be ready always to give an answer to every man that asketh you a reason of the hope that is in you with meekness and fear." This verse emphasizes the importance of being prepared to explain and defend your beliefs in a respectful and confident manner.

Improving your understanding of the faith involves regular study of the Bible, as well as reading other theological works and engaging in discussions with knowledgeable Christians. This deepens your knowledge of key doctrines, biblical history, and the reasons behind your beliefs, which is essential for effectively sharing your faith. Just as a pitcher studies different pitches and techniques, Christians should study different aspects of their faith to be well-rounded and knowledgeable. Communicating your faith clearly requires practice and the development of effective communication skills. This might involve practicing how to share your testimony, explain key doctrines, or respond to common questions and objections about Christianity. Role-playing with friends or mentors can be a helpful way to refine your ability to articulate your beliefs. Just as a pitcher practices different pitches, Christians can practice different ways of sharing their faith to be more effective in various situations.

Confidence in sharing your faith comes from a deep conviction in what you believe and the assurance that comes from a personal relationship with God. This confidence can be strengthened through prayer, worship, and regular engagement with the Christian community. Being part of a supportive church family can provide encouragement and opportunities to practice sharing your faith in a safe environment. Just as a pitcher gains confidence from successful practice sessions and positive feedback from coaches, Christians can gain confidence from positive experiences of sharing their faith and the encouragement of fellow believers. Defending your faith involves being able to respond to challenges and criticisms with grace and truth. This requires not only knowledge but also wisdom and discernment. Learning from apologists and engaging in apologetics can equip you with the tools needed to address difficult questions and objections. Just as a pitcher prepares for tough batters by understanding their strengths and weaknesses, Christians can prepare for challenging conversations by understanding common objections to the faith and how to address them thoughtfully and respectfully.

In addition to individual practice, being part of a community that values and supports evangelism is important. Just as a pitcher benefits from being part of a team, Christians benefit from being part of a church that encourages sharing the gospel and provides resources and training for evangelism. This communal support can help you stay motivated and accountable in your efforts to share your faith. In conclusion, improving pitching skills by focusing on mechanics, control, and velocity is essential for a successful baseball pitcher, just as developing the ability to share and defend your faith with clarity and confidence is crucial for a strong Christian witness. Both require dedication, practice, and a willingness to learn and grow. By committing to these practices, whether on the baseball field or in your spiritual life, you can become more effective and impactful. The principles of preparation, practice, and confidence are key to success in both areas, helping you to excel and make a positive difference.

Chapter 9 - Enhance Fielding Abilities

"Whatsoever thy hand findeth to do, do it with thy might."
Ecclesiastes 9:10

Enhancing fielding abilities is crucial for any baseball player who wants to excel on the field. This involves practicing fielding ground balls, catching fly balls, and making accurate throws consistently. Fielding ground balls requires agility, quick reflexes, and proper technique to scoop the ball cleanly and transfer it quickly to your throwing hand. Players should practice getting into a ready position, staying low, and using both hands to field the ball effectively. Drills that involve fielding balls hit at various speeds and angles can help improve these skills. Catching fly balls is another essential aspect of fielding. It requires good hand-eye coordination, speed, and the ability to judge the trajectory of the ball. Practicing catching fly balls in different conditions, such as under the sun or with a high sky, can help players become more reliable outfielders. Making accurate throws is vital for completing plays and preventing runners from advancing. This involves having a strong arm, a quick release, and the ability to throw accurately from different positions on the field. Drills that focus on throwing mechanics, such as the crow hop technique, and practicing long throws can improve accuracy and strength. Overall, regular practice, attention to detail, and a commitment to improvement are key to enhancing fielding abilities. By focusing on these skills, a player can become a more dependable and effective fielder, contributing significantly to the team's success.

In the life of a Christian, being diligent in your spiritual duties and responsibilities is just as important as practicing fielding skills is for a baseball player. The Bible verse Ecclesiastes 9:10 says, "Whatsoever thy hand findeth to do, do it with thy might." This verse emphasizes the importance of giving your best effort in all tasks, including your spiritual responsibilities. Christians have various duties and responsibilities, such as prayer, reading the Bible, attending church, serving others, and living a life that reflects the teachings of Jesus Christ. Being diligent in these areas means approaching them with dedication, focus, and a desire to honor God.

Prayer is a fundamental spiritual duty that involves communicating with God, expressing gratitude, seeking guidance, and interceding for others. To be diligent in prayer, Christians should set aside regular time each day for focused prayer, create a quiet environment free from distractions, and approach God with sincerity and humility. Developing a consistent prayer routine helps to deepen one's relationship with God and provides a strong foundation for spiritual growth.

Reading the Bible is another essential responsibility. The Bible is the primary source of God's Word and provides guidance, wisdom, and encouragement. Regular Bible study helps Christians understand God's commandments, grow in faith, and apply biblical principles to their daily lives. Being diligent in Bible reading involves setting aside dedicated time each day to read and meditate on scripture, using study aids such as commentaries and devotionals, and seeking to understand and apply the lessons learned.

Attending church and participating in the life of the church community is also important. Church provides a place for worship, fellowship, and spiritual nourishment. Being diligent in church attendance means making it a priority to attend services regularly, participating in church activities and ministries, and building relationships with other believers. This commitment to the church community helps Christians grow in their faith, find support and encouragement, and serve others.

Serving others is a key aspect of the Christian life. Jesus taught that serving others is a way to demonstrate God's love and reflect His character. Being diligent in serving others involves looking for opportunities to help those in need, using your gifts and talents to benefit others, and approaching service with a willing and joyful heart. This can include volunteering at church or in the community, helping a neighbor, or supporting charitable organizations.

Living a life that reflects the teachings of Jesus Christ is the overarching responsibility of every Christian. This means striving to live according to biblical principles, such as love, kindness, honesty, and integrity. Being diligent in this area involves regularly examining your actions and attitudes, seeking to grow in character, and being a positive example to others. It also means being mindful of your witness and striving to share your faith through both words and actions.

In conclusion, enhancing fielding abilities by practicing fielding ground balls, catching fly balls, and making accurate throws is essential for a successful baseball player, just as being diligent in your spiritual duties and responsibilities is crucial for a strong Christian life. Both require dedication, practice, and a commitment to excellence. By focusing on these skills and responsibilities, whether on the baseball field or in your spiritual walk, you can achieve greater success and fulfillment. The principles of diligence, consistency, and wholehearted effort are key to excelling in both areas, helping you to grow and thrive in your pursuits.

Chapter 10 - Base Running Skills

"Wherefore seeing we also are compassed about with so great a cloud of witnesses, let us lay aside every weight, and the sin which doth so easily beset us, and let us run with patience the race that is set before us." Hebrews 12:1

To excel as a baseball player, mastering the fundamentals of base running is essential, encompassing skills like stealing bases and sliding techniques. Base running goes beyond mere speed; it involves strategic thinking, precise timing, and flawless technique. Stealing bases, for example, demands quick reflexes, a deep understanding of the pitcher's patterns, and impeccable timing. This skill requires players to take an optimal lead-off, attentively observe the pitcher's movements, and then sprint to the next base at the exact right moment. Regular practice of these elements, including running drills and simulated game situations, hones these skills and boosts a player's confidence and proficiency in stealing bases. Sliding techniques are equally crucial in base running. Knowing how to slide properly can make the difference between being safe or out at a base. There are different sliding methods, such as the head-first slide and the feet-first slide, each suitable for different scenarios. Practicing these slides repeatedly ensures that players can perform them safely and effectively during a game. Additionally, players must understand base running signals from coaches, anticipate fielders' throws, and make split-second decisions on whether to take an extra base or hold up. This comprehensive understanding and execution of base running can turn a good player into a great one, significantly contributing to the team's overall success.

In the life of a Christian, running your spiritual race with endurance and purpose is just as vital. The Bible verse Hebrews 12:1 states, "Wherefore seeing we also are compassed about with so great a cloud of witnesses, let us lay aside every weight, and the sin which doth so easily beset us, and let us run with patience the race that is set before us." This verse emphasizes the importance of perseverance, focus, and removing obstacles in our spiritual journey. Just as base running in baseball requires discipline, strategy, and practice, running the spiritual race requires dedication, purpose, and endurance. Endurance in the spiritual race means maintaining faith and commitment even when faced with challenges, difficulties, and temptations. It involves staying focused on God's promises and purposes and not giving up when the journey gets tough. Christians are encouraged to draw strength from the example of those who have gone before them—the "great cloud of witnesses" mentioned in Hebrews 12:1. These witnesses are the heroes of faith whose lives are recorded in the Bible, and their stories serve as inspiration and encouragement for believers today.

Running with purpose means having a clear understanding of your spiritual goals and the direction God has for your life. Just as a base runner must know the layout of the bases and the rules of the game, Christians must understand their faith, God's commandments, and His will for their lives. This understanding comes from regular study of the Bible, prayer, and seeking guidance from the Holy Spirit. It also involves being part of a faith community where you can receive support, accountability, and encouragement from other believers. Removing obstacles, such as sin and distractions, is crucial for running the spiritual race effectively. Just as a baseball player needs to avoid errors and distractions to run the bases successfully, Christians need to identify and remove anything that hinders their relationship with God and their spiritual progress. This might involve confessing and repenting of sin, setting healthy boundaries, and making intentional choices to focus on what is important. Laying aside these weights allows for a more focused and effective spiritual journey.

Patience is another important aspect of the spiritual race. Just as base running requires timing and patience, waiting for the right moment to steal a base or advance, Christians need to cultivate patience in their walk with God. This means trusting in God's timing, being patient in affliction, and persevering in faith even when answers to prayers are delayed or circumstances are challenging. Patience helps to build character and deepen faith, making believers more resilient and mature in their spiritual journey. In conclusion, learning the fundamentals of base running, including stealing bases and sliding techniques, is essential for a successful baseball player, just as running your spiritual race with endurance and purpose is crucial for a strong Christian life. Both require discipline, strategy, and a commitment to continual improvement. By focusing on these skills and responsibilities, whether on the baseball field or in your spiritual walk, you can achieve greater success and fulfillment. The principles of perseverance, focus, and removing obstacles are key to excelling in both areas, helping you to grow and thrive in your pursuits. Whether navigating the bases or your spiritual journey, the commitment to running with purpose and endurance leads to victory and a fulfilling life.

Chapter 11 - Watch Professional Games

"Brethren, be followers together of me, and mark them which walk so as ye have us for an ensample." - Philippians 3:17

To become a better baseball player, one of the most effective methods is to watch professional games and observe the players to learn advanced techniques and strategies. Watching the pros play gives you an up-close view of how the best in the sport perform under pressure, handle different game situations, and execute skills with precision. By carefully observing professional players, you can pick up on their batting stances, pitching styles, fielding techniques, and base-running tactics. You can see how they adjust their strategies depending on the game's context, such as the score, inning, or opposing team's strengths and weaknesses. For instance, watching a skilled pitcher can teach you about different grips and pitches, how to read batters, and how to maintain composure on the mound. Observing batters can reveal how they handle different types of pitches, their approach to different counts, and how they adjust their swings based on the situation. Fielders demonstrate how to position themselves, react quickly to hits, and make accurate throws. Base runners showcase timing, speed, and decision-making skills that can be crucial in tight situations. By watching these professionals, you can learn the subtle nuances of the game that are often not covered in basic training. Additionally, watching games can help you understand the mental aspects of baseball, such as staying focused, handling pressure, and maintaining a positive attitude even when things aren't going well. It's beneficial to take notes, discuss observations with coaches or teammates, and try to implement what you've learned during practice and games. This method of learning by observation helps to bridge the gap between theory and practice, making you a more well-rounded and knowledgeable player.

In the life of a Christian, observing the lives of mature believers and learning from their examples is equally important. The Bible verse Philippians 3:17 says, "Brethren, be followers together of me, and mark them which walk so as ye have us for an ensample." This verse highlights the value of looking up to mature Christians who exemplify a faithful walk with God. Just as watching professional baseball players helps improve your game, observing the lives of mature Christians can provide invaluable lessons for your spiritual journey. These individuals often embody the principles of faith, love, patience, and perseverance that are essential for a strong Christian life. By watching how they navigate their faith, deal with challenges, and serve others, you can gain practical insights into living out your beliefs.

Mature Christians often have a deep understanding of the Bible, a strong prayer life, and a commitment to serving others, which are qualities that can inspire and guide you. For example, observing how they study and interpret the Bible can help you develop better study habits and gain deeper insights into scripture. Watching their prayer life can teach you the importance of regular and sincere communication with God, and how to pray effectively. Seeing how they serve others can motivate you to find your own ways to contribute to your community and church. Their responses to difficult situations can show you how to trust in God, remain faithful, and find peace even in times of trouble. Just as professional athletes demonstrate the highest level of skill in their sport, mature Christians demonstrate the highest level of faith in their walk with God.

Being part of a church community where you can observe and interact with mature Christians is essential for this learning process. It provides opportunities for mentorship, where more experienced believers can offer guidance, support, and encouragement. Small groups, Bible studies, and church activities are all environments where you can learn from others' experiences and share your own. This mutual support helps to build a stronger, more vibrant faith community. Furthermore, learning from mature Christians helps you to avoid common pitfalls and mistakes in your spiritual journey. Just as young baseball players can learn what to do and what not to do by watching the pros, young Christians can learn valuable lessons by observing the lives of those who have walked the path of faith before them. This can include learning how to deal with doubt, handle criticism, and maintain integrity and honesty in all situations.

In conclusion, watching professional baseball games to observe advanced techniques and strategies is a powerful way to improve as a player, just as observing the lives of mature Christians and learning from their examples is crucial for growing in faith. Both practices involve learning from those who have more experience and have demonstrated excellence in their field. By watching and emulating their skills and behaviors, whether on the baseball field or in your spiritual walk, you can develop the knowledge, skills, and character needed to succeed and thrive. The principles of observation, learning, and applying what you see are key to excelling in both baseball and the Christian life. By incorporating these practices into your routine, you can become a more skilled and knowledgeable player and a more faithful and committed Christian.

Chapter 12 - Get Coaching

"Where no counsel is, the people fall: but in the multitude of counsellors there is safety." Proverbs 11:14

To become a successful baseball player, seeking guidance from experienced coaches is essential for refining your skills and strategy. Coaches bring a wealth of knowledge and expertise that can significantly enhance your understanding of the game and help you improve your performance. By working with a coach, you can receive personalized feedback on your technique, whether it's your batting stance, pitching mechanics, or fielding position. A coach can identify areas where you need improvement and provide specific drills and exercises to help you address those weaknesses. They can also help you develop a game strategy, teaching you how to read the game, anticipate plays, and make smart decisions on the field. Additionally, coaches can offer valuable insights into the mental aspects of baseball, such as staying focused, maintaining confidence, and handling pressure. Regular practice sessions with a coach allow you to continuously refine your skills, learn new techniques, and build a deeper understanding of the game. The guidance and support of a coach can make a significant difference in your development as a player, helping you reach your full potential and achieve your goals. Being open to feedback and willing to work hard to implement your coach's advice are crucial aspects of this process. The relationship between a player and coach is built on trust, respect, and a shared commitment to improvement.

In the life of a Christian, seeking mentorship from spiritual leaders and mature believers is equally important. The Bible verse Proverbs 11:14 says, "Where no counsel is, the people fall: but in the multitude of counsellors there is safety." This verse highlights the importance of seeking guidance and wisdom from those who have more experience and understanding. Just as a baseball player benefits from the expertise of a coach, Christians benefit from the mentorship of spiritual leaders and mature believers who can provide guidance, support, and encouragement in their faith journey. Spiritual mentors can help you grow in your understanding of the Bible, deepen your prayer life, and live out your faith in practical ways. They can offer insights into how to apply biblical principles to everyday situations, helping you navigate challenges and make decisions that honor God. Mentors can also provide accountability, helping you stay committed to your spiritual goals and avoid pitfalls. They can share their own experiences and lessons learned, providing valuable examples of faithful living. Regular meetings with a mentor, whether through one-on-one sessions, small group discussions, or church activities, can provide a supportive environment for spiritual growth and development.

Being part of a church community is essential for finding and building these mentoring relationships. Church activities such as Bible studies, prayer groups, and fellowship events provide opportunities to connect with mature believers who can offer guidance and support. These interactions help to build a network of relationships where you can receive counsel, encouragement, and accountability. Just as a baseball player needs a coach to guide their development, Christians need spiritual mentors to help them grow in their faith and navigate the challenges of life. Mentorship also involves a willingness to be open and teachable. Just as a baseball player must be willing to receive feedback and work on their weaknesses, Christians must be willing to listen to their mentors, reflect on their advice, and make changes as needed. This humility and openness to learning are essential for growth and development. By seeking mentorship and being receptive to guidance, you can gain valuable insights and grow stronger in your faith.

In addition to personal mentorship, learning from the collective wisdom of the Christian community is also important. The multitude of counsellors mentioned in Proverbs 11:14 highlights the value of receiving input from a variety of sources. This can include attending church services, listening to sermons, reading Christian books, and participating in conferences and workshops. Each of these sources can provide different perspectives and insights, enriching your understanding and helping you grow in your faith.

The benefits of seeking coaching or mentorship are numerous. In baseball, coaches help players improve their technical skills, understand the game's strategies, and develop the mental toughness needed to succeed. This support is invaluable in helping players reach their full potential and perform at their best. In the Christian life, spiritual mentors provide guidance on how to live out one's faith, offer support during difficult times, and help believers grow in their relationship with God. This guidance helps Christians navigate the complexities of life with wisdom and faith, staying true to their beliefs and values. Both coaching and mentorship require commitment and active participation. In baseball, players must be dedicated to attending practices, listening to their coaches, and putting in the hard work needed to improve. Similarly, in the Christian life, believers must be committed to their spiritual growth, willing to seek out and follow the advice of their mentors, and dedicated to living out their faith in all aspects of their lives.

In conclusion, getting coaching from experienced coaches is crucial for refining your skills and strategy as a baseball player, just as seeking mentorship from spiritual leaders and mature believers is essential for growing in your faith as a Christian. Both require a commitment to learning, a willingness to receive feedback, and a dedication to continuous improvement. By seeking guidance from those with more experience and wisdom, whether on the baseball field or in your spiritual life, you can develop the skills and understanding needed to succeed and thrive. The principles of mentorship, guidance, and learning from others are key to excelling in both areas, helping you to reach your full potential and live a fulfilling and impactful life.

Chapter 13 - Play in Various Positions

"I can do all things through Christ which strengtheneth me."
Philippians 4:13

To become a well-rounded and successful baseball player, it's important to gain versatility by playing in various positions on the field. Playing in different positions allows you to develop a broad range of skills and a deeper understanding of the game. Each position on the baseball field requires different techniques, perspectives, and strategies. For example, playing in the infield involves quick reflexes, accurate throws, and the ability to field ground balls, while playing in the outfield requires speed, the ability to judge fly balls, and a strong throwing arm. By experiencing different positions, you can become more adaptable and valuable to your team. This versatility allows you to step in wherever needed, making you a more flexible and indispensable player. It also helps you to understand the responsibilities and challenges of each position, fostering a greater appreciation for your teammates' roles and improving overall team dynamics. Coaches often value players who can fill multiple roles because it provides more options during games and helps cover for injuries or strategic changes. Additionally, learning to play various positions can help you discover your strengths and preferences, guiding you toward the position where you can excel the most. Practicing in different positions also keeps your training dynamic and engaging, preventing monotony and encouraging continuous learning. Overall, gaining versatility on the field enhances your skill set, makes you a more complete player, and increases your contributions to the team's success.

In the life of a Christian, being willing to serve in various capacities within the church and community is just as important. The Bible verse Philippians 4:13 says, "I can do all things through Christ which strengtheneth me." This verse emphasizes the strength and capability that come from Christ, enabling believers to serve in different roles and meet various needs. Just as a versatile baseball player is valuable to their team, a Christian who is willing to serve in multiple ways is a great asset to their church and community. Serving in different capacities allows you to use and develop a wide range of talents and skills. It also helps you to grow spiritually, as each service opportunity can teach you new lessons about faith, humility, and love.

Being open to serving in various roles means being flexible and ready to step out of your comfort zone. In a church setting, this might involve helping with different ministries such as teaching Sunday school, participating in the worship team, assisting with community outreach programs, or supporting administrative tasks. Each role, though different, contributes to the overall mission of the church and provides valuable experiences and growth opportunities. Serving in the community can include volunteering at local shelters, participating in charity events, mentoring youth, or supporting local initiatives. These acts of service not only meet practical needs but also demonstrate Christ's love to others and build stronger community bonds.

Serving in various capacities also helps you understand and appreciate the different functions within the church and community. Just as playing different positions on the baseball field gives you insight into the game, serving in different roles gives you a broader perspective on how the church operates and the diverse ways God's work is carried out. It fosters a sense of unity and teamwork, as you recognize that each role, no matter how small it may seem, is important and valuable. This willingness to serve in different areas reflects a heart of humility and a desire to be used by God wherever needed.

Furthermore, being versatile in your service allows you to discover and develop your spiritual gifts. The Bible teaches that each believer is given unique gifts by the Holy Spirit to serve others and build up the body of Christ. By trying out different roles, you can identify your strengths and passions, which can guide you in finding your most effective and fulfilling place of service. This not only benefits the church and community but also brings personal satisfaction and joy as you see how God can use you in various ways.

In conclusion, playing in various positions on the baseball field helps you become a more versatile and valuable player, just as being willing to serve in various capacities within the church and community helps you become a more effective and impactful Christian. Both require a willingness to step out of your comfort zone, learn new skills, and adapt to different situations. By embracing versatility, whether in baseball or in your spiritual life, you can contribute more fully to your team and community, grow personally and spiritually, and experience the fulfillment that comes from serving others. The principles of flexibility, willingness to learn, and commitment to service are key to excelling in both areas, helping you to reach your full potential and make a positive difference in the world around you.

Chapter 14 - Set Goals

"I press toward the mark for the prize of the high calling of God in Christ Jesus." Philippians 3:14

To become a successful baseball player, setting goals is essential for staying motivated and focused. Establishing both short-term and long-term goals helps you to measure progress, maintain direction, and achieve success on the field. Short-term goals might include improving your batting average, mastering a new pitching technique, or increasing your speed on the bases. These goals are specific, measurable, and achievable within a relatively short period, providing immediate targets to aim for. By setting short-term goals, you can see regular progress, which boosts confidence and keeps you motivated. Long-term goals, on the other hand, provide a broader vision for your baseball career. These might include making the varsity team, earning a college scholarship, or even playing professionally. Long-term goals require sustained effort and commitment, serving as a constant reminder of what you're working toward. Together, short-term and long-term goals create a roadmap for your development as a player. They help you to prioritize your training, focus on areas that need improvement, and stay committed to your practice schedule. By regularly reviewing and adjusting your goals, you can ensure that you're always moving forward and making the most of your abilities. Coaches and mentors can also play a crucial role in helping you set realistic goals and develop a plan to achieve them. By setting and pursuing these goals, you can stay motivated, focused, and on track to reach your full potential as a baseball player.

In the life of a Christian, setting spiritual goals is equally important for growing in faith and service. The Bible verse Philippians 3:14 says, "I press toward the mark for the prize of the high calling of God in Christ Jesus." This verse emphasizes the importance of having a clear goal and striving towards it with dedication and perseverance. Just as setting goals in baseball helps you to improve and succeed, setting spiritual goals helps you to grow in your relationship with God and your ability to serve others. Spiritual goals might include reading the Bible regularly, deepening your prayer life, participating more actively in church, or finding ways to serve your community. By setting these goals, you create a clear path for your spiritual growth and ensure that you're making progress in your faith journey.

Short-term spiritual goals could include committing to a daily Bible reading plan, joining a small group for fellowship and study, or volunteering for a church ministry. These goals are achievable in the near term and provide immediate steps to deepen your faith and connect with others. Achieving short-term goals can provide a sense of accomplishment and encourage you to continue pursuing further growth. Long-term spiritual goals might involve developing a deeper understanding of theology, going on a mission trip, or becoming a mentor to others in their faith. These goals require ongoing commitment and effort, helping you to grow steadily over time and make a significant impact in your community and beyond.

Setting and pursuing spiritual goals also helps you to stay focused on your relationship with God. It reminds you of the importance of dedicating time and effort to spiritual practices, even amidst the busyness of daily life. Just as a baseball player needs to prioritize training to improve, a Christian needs to prioritize spiritual disciplines to grow in faith. Setting goals helps to keep you accountable and ensures that you're continually moving forward in your spiritual journey.

Additionally, sharing your goals with a mentor, accountability partner, or faith community can provide support and encouragement. Just as coaches and teammates can help you stay on track with your baseball goals, fellow believers can offer guidance, prayer, and encouragement as you pursue your spiritual goals. This support network can help you stay motivated and overcome challenges along the way.

Both in baseball and in the Christian life, setting goals provides a clear sense of direction and purpose. It helps you to focus your efforts, measure your progress, and celebrate your achievements. By setting goals, you ensure that you're always working towards something meaningful and striving to reach your full potential. Whether you're aiming to improve your skills on the baseball field or deepen your faith and service to others, having clear goals provides the motivation and focus needed to succeed.

In conclusion, setting goals is crucial for staying motivated and focused as a baseball player, just as setting spiritual goals is essential for growing in faith and service as a Christian. Both require a clear vision, commitment, and regular effort. By establishing short-term and long-term goals, you can create a roadmap for success, track your progress, and stay motivated even when faced with challenges. The principles of goal-setting, perseverance, and dedication are key to excelling in both areas, helping you to reach your full potential and live a fulfilling and impactful life. Whether on the baseball field or in your spiritual journey, setting and pursuing goals allows you to achieve your dreams and make a positive difference in the world around you.

15. **Analyze Your Performance**: Regularly review your games to identify areas for improvement.

Christian Application: Reflect on your spiritual journey to identify strengths and areas for growth.

Verse: "Examine yourselves, whether ye be in the faith; prove your own selves." - 2 Corinthians 13:5

To become a successful baseball player, it's crucial to analyze your performance regularly. This means taking the time to review your games, practices, and overall performance to identify areas where you can improve. Analyzing your performance involves looking at various aspects of your game, such as your batting average, pitching accuracy, fielding skills, and base running. By doing this, you can pinpoint specific weaknesses that need attention and work on strategies to overcome them. For instance, if you notice that your batting average is lower than you'd like, you can work on your swing mechanics, timing, and pitch selection. If your pitching accuracy needs improvement, you can focus on refining your pitching techniques, like your grip and release. Reviewing game footage can be particularly helpful as it allows you to see yourself in action, understand your mistakes, and learn from them. It's also beneficial to seek feedback from coaches and teammates, as they can provide valuable insights and suggestions for improvement. Regularly analyzing your performance helps you stay motivated and focused on your goals, ensuring that you're constantly working to become a better player. This process of self-reflection and continuous improvement is essential for achieving success on the field. In the life of a Christian, reflecting on your spiritual journey is equally important. The Bible verse 2 Corinthians 13:5 says, "Examine yourselves, whether ye be in the faith; prove your own selves." This verse emphasizes the importance of self-examination and reflection in the Christian life. Just as analyzing your performance in baseball helps you identify areas for improvement, reflecting on your spiritual journey helps you recognize your strengths and areas where you need to grow. This reflection involves looking at various aspects of your faith life, such as your relationship with God, your prayer life, your understanding of the Bible, and your interactions with others. By doing this, you can identify specific areas where you need to focus your efforts.

For example, if you find that your prayer life has been lacking, you can set aside more time each day for prayer and meditation. If you feel that your understanding of the Bible could be deeper, you can commit to regular Bible study and seek guidance from knowledgeable mentors. Reflecting on your spiritual journey also means acknowledging your strengths and celebrating the progress you've made. This helps to keep you motivated and encouraged as you continue to grow in your faith.

Seeking feedback from spiritual mentors, pastors, and fellow believers can be incredibly beneficial. Just as coaches and teammates provide insights into your baseball performance, spiritual mentors can offer valuable perspectives on your faith journey. They can help you see areas where you might be blind to your own weaknesses and provide guidance on how to grow and improve. Regular self-examination and reflection ensure that you're constantly striving to deepen your relationship with God and live out your faith more fully.

In both baseball and the Christian life, the process of analyzing your performance and reflecting on your journey requires honesty, humility, and a willingness to change. It's not always easy to acknowledge your weaknesses and areas where you need to improve, but doing so is essential for growth and development. By regularly reviewing your performance and reflecting on your journey, you can stay on track, set meaningful goals, and make continuous progress.

In conclusion, analyzing your performance regularly is essential for becoming a successful baseball player, just as reflecting on your spiritual journey is crucial for growing in your faith as a Christian. Both require a commitment to self-examination, a willingness to receive feedback, and a dedication to continuous improvement. By regularly reviewing your games and identifying areas for improvement, you can become a better player and achieve your goals on the field. Similarly, by reflecting on your spiritual journey and identifying areas for growth, you can deepen your relationship with God and live out your faith more fully. The principles of self-examination, reflection, and continuous improvement are key to excelling in both areas, helping you to reach your full potential and live a fulfilling and impactful life. Whether on the baseball field or in your spiritual journey, regular analysis and reflection allow you to achieve your dreams and make a positive difference in the world around you.

Chapter 16 - Nutrition and Hydration

"It is written, Man shall not live by bread alone, but by every word that proceedeth out of the mouth of God." Matthew 4:4

Maintaining a healthy diet and staying hydrated are essential for optimizing performance as a baseball player. Good nutrition provides the energy and nutrients your body needs to perform at its best, whether you're practicing, playing in a game, or recovering afterward. A balanced diet for an athlete includes a variety of foods from all the major food groups: carbohydrates for energy, proteins for muscle repair and growth, healthy fats for sustained energy, as well as vitamins and minerals to support overall health. Carbohydrates, such as whole grains, fruits, and vegetables, are particularly important for providing the quick energy needed during intense physical activity. Proteins, found in lean meats, beans, and dairy products, help to repair and build muscle tissues that are stressed and broken down during workouts and games. Healthy fats, like those in nuts, seeds, and avocados, provide long-lasting energy and help with hormone production. Eating a variety of nutrient-dense foods ensures that your body gets the fuel it needs to function optimally. In addition to eating a balanced diet, staying hydrated is crucial. Water is essential for maintaining body temperature, removing waste, and lubricating joints. Dehydration can lead to fatigue, muscle cramps, and decreased performance, so it's important to drink plenty of water before, during, and after physical activity. Sports drinks can also be useful for replenishing electrolytes lost through sweat during intense exercise. Consistently maintaining good nutrition and hydration habits can improve your endurance, strength, and overall performance on the field.

In the life of a Christian, nourishing your soul with the Word of God and staying spiritually hydrated is just as important. The Bible verse Matthew 4:4 says, "It is written, Man shall not live by bread alone, but by every word that proceedeth out of the mouth of God." This verse highlights the necessity of spiritual nourishment, which is as crucial to the soul as physical food and water are to the body. Just as athletes need a balanced diet to perform well, Christians need a steady intake of God's Word to grow and thrive in their faith. Reading the Bible regularly provides spiritual sustenance, offering guidance, wisdom, and encouragement. The scriptures are full of teachings that help believers understand God's will, navigate life's challenges, and grow in their relationship with Him. By spending time in the Word, Christians can strengthen their faith, gain a deeper understanding of God's character, and find direction for their lives.

In addition to reading the Bible, prayer is another vital aspect of spiritual nourishment. Prayer is a way to communicate with God, express gratitude, seek guidance, and intercede for others. It helps to maintain a close and personal relationship with God, providing spiritual hydration that refreshes and revitalizes the soul. Regular prayer helps believers to stay connected with God, draw strength from Him, and remain grounded in their faith.

Attending church services and participating in fellowship with other believers also play a crucial role in spiritual nourishment. Being part of a faith community provides support, encouragement, and accountability. It allows Christians to worship together, share their experiences, and grow in their faith collectively. Fellowship with other believers helps to strengthen the sense of community and provides opportunities for mutual support and growth.

Just as an athlete needs to avoid junk food and unhealthy habits to maintain optimal performance, Christians need to avoid spiritual "junk food" that can hinder their growth. This includes anything that distracts from or undermines their relationship with God, such as negative influences, sinful behaviors, or distractions that take time away from spiritual practices. By focusing on what nourishes the soul and avoiding what doesn't, believers can maintain a healthy and vibrant spiritual life.

In conclusion, maintaining a healthy diet and staying hydrated are essential for optimizing performance as a baseball player, just as nourishing your soul with the Word of God and staying spiritually hydrated are crucial for a strong Christian life. Both require a commitment to regular, healthy habits and a focus on what truly sustains and strengthens. By prioritizing good nutrition and hydration, athletes can improve their endurance, strength, and overall performance. Similarly, by prioritizing spiritual nourishment through the Word of God, prayer, and fellowship, Christians can grow in their faith, stay connected with God, and live out their beliefs more fully. The principles of regular nourishment, avoiding harmful influences, and maintaining healthy habits are key to excelling in both areas, helping you to reach your full potential and live a fulfilling and impactful life. Whether on the baseball field or in your spiritual journey, consistent attention to what you consume and how you nourish yourself can lead to greater success and fulfillment.

Chapter 17 - Rest and Recovery

"Come unto me, all ye that labour and are heavy laden, and I will give you rest." Matthew 11:28

To become a successful baseball player, ensuring you get adequate rest and recovery is crucial for preventing injuries and maintaining peak performance. Rest and recovery are essential components of any training program, as they allow your body to heal, rebuild, and strengthen after intense physical activity. Without proper rest, you risk overtraining, which can lead to fatigue, decreased performance, and a higher likelihood of injuries such as strains, sprains, and stress fractures. Adequate sleep is a vital part of rest and recovery. During sleep, your body repairs muscle tissues, replenishes energy stores, and releases growth hormones that contribute to muscle growth and overall recovery. Aim for 7-9 hours of quality sleep each night to support these processes. In addition to sleep, incorporating rest days into your training schedule is important. Rest days give your muscles and joints a break from the repetitive strain of intense workouts and games, allowing them to recover and reduce the risk of injury. Active recovery, such as light jogging, stretching, or yoga, can also be beneficial. These low-intensity activities help increase blood flow to the muscles, aiding in the removal of waste products and reducing muscle soreness. Nutrition plays a role in recovery as well. Consuming a balanced diet rich in proteins, carbohydrates, and healthy fats provides the necessary nutrients for muscle repair and energy restoration. Hydration is equally important, as staying properly hydrated helps maintain bodily functions and supports recovery processes. Another aspect of recovery is mental rest. Engaging in activities that relax your mind, such as reading, listening to music, or spending time with family and friends, can help reduce stress and improve overall well-being. By prioritizing rest and recovery, you allow your body to perform at its best, enhance your endurance, and extend your athletic career. In the life of a Christian, resting in the Lord and finding spiritual renewal in Him is equally important. The Bible verse Matthew 11:28 says, "Come unto me, all ye that labour and are heavy laden, and I will give you rest." This verse emphasizes the importance of seeking rest and renewal in God, especially when feeling burdened or weary. Just as athletes need physical rest to perform well, Christians need spiritual rest to maintain a healthy and vibrant faith life. Spiritual rest involves taking time to pause, reflect, and connect with God. It means setting aside regular time for prayer, meditation, and reading the Bible. These practices help to rejuvenate your spirit, provide clarity and peace, and strengthen your relationship with God. In prayer, you can lay down your burdens, seek God's guidance, and find comfort in His presence. Meditation on scripture allows you to absorb God's Word deeply, drawing wisdom and encouragement from His promises. Reading the Bible regularly helps you to stay grounded in your faith, gain insight into God's will, and find direction for your life. Attending church and participating in worship also provide opportunities for spiritual rest and renewal. Corporate worship allows you to join with other believers in praising God, which can be uplifting and revitalizing. The fellowship and community support found in church can also provide encouragement and strength. Just as physical rest helps to restore your body, spiritual rest helps to restore your soul. It's important to recognize when you need to step back from the busyness of life and take time to rest in God's presence. This might involve taking a break from certain activities, spending quiet time in nature, or simply sitting in silence with God.

Balancing work, responsibilities, and rest is essential for a healthy life. Overcommitting and neglecting rest can lead to burnout, stress, and a weakened spiritual life. Just as athletes schedule rest days to prevent overtraining, Christians should schedule regular times for spiritual rest to prevent spiritual exhaustion. Trusting in God's promise of rest means believing that He will provide for your needs and that taking time to rest is not a sign of weakness, but a necessary part of a healthy and balanced life. In conclusion, ensuring adequate rest and recovery is essential for preventing injuries and maintaining peak performance as a baseball player, just as resting in the Lord and finding spiritual renewal in Him is crucial for a strong Christian life. Both require a commitment to recognizing the importance of rest and taking intentional steps to incorporate it into your routine. By prioritizing rest and recovery, athletes can enhance their performance, reduce the risk of injury, and enjoy a longer athletic career. Similarly, by prioritizing spiritual rest and renewal, Christians can maintain a vibrant faith, find peace and strength in God, and live a fulfilling and impactful life. The principles of rest, renewal, and balance are key to excelling in both areas, helping you to reach your full potential and live a healthy, joyful life. Whether on the baseball field or in your spiritual journey, taking time to rest and recover allows you to be at your best, ready to face challenges with energy, focus, and a refreshed spirit.

Chapter 18 - Build Team Chemistry

"Behold, how good and how pleasant it is for brethren to dwell together in unity!" Psalm 133:1

To become a successful baseball player, building team chemistry is crucial. This means working on developing good relationships with your teammates and understanding team dynamics. Team chemistry involves trust, communication, and a sense of camaraderie that allows the team to work together effectively and achieve common goals. Good relationships among teammates can lead to better coordination on the field, more efficient practices, and a more positive and supportive team environment. Building team chemistry starts with getting to know your teammates personally, both on and off the field. This can involve spending time together outside of practice, engaging in team-building activities, and supporting each other through challenges and successes. Effective communication is key to good team chemistry. This means not only talking to each other but also listening and understanding different perspectives. Encouraging open and honest communication helps to resolve conflicts, clarify misunderstandings, and build a strong sense of unity. Trust is another essential component. Trusting your teammates to perform their roles and supporting them in their efforts fosters a sense of reliability and confidence. Team chemistry also involves understanding each player's strengths and weaknesses and finding ways to complement each other's skills. By working together and supporting each other, the team can function as a cohesive unit, enhancing overall performance and achieving success on the field.

In the life of a Christian, building strong relationships with fellow believers and fostering unity in the church is equally important. The Bible verse Psalm 133:1 says, "Behold, how good and how pleasant it is for brethren to dwell together in unity!" This verse emphasizes the value of unity and harmonious relationships among believers. Just as team chemistry is crucial for a successful baseball team, unity and strong relationships are vital for a thriving church community. Building these relationships involves getting to know fellow church members, spending time together in fellowship, and supporting each other in faith and life's challenges. Church activities such as small groups, prayer meetings, and social events provide opportunities to connect with others and build meaningful relationships.

Effective communication is also important in the church. Open and honest communication helps to build trust, resolve conflicts, and ensure that everyone feels heard and valued. Encouraging dialogue and understanding different perspectives can strengthen the sense of community and unity within the church. Trust is essential in church relationships as well. Trusting each other to uphold shared values and support one another in times of need builds a strong foundation for unity. Understanding and appreciating each other's spiritual gifts and talents can help to create a more cohesive and effective church community. By working together and supporting each other, the church can fulfill its mission more effectively and provide a welcoming and nurturing environment for all its members.

Building unity in the church also involves fostering a spirit of love and acceptance. This means welcoming newcomers, being inclusive, and showing kindness and compassion to all members. Encouraging and supporting each other in faith journeys helps to build a strong and united church community. Just as a baseball team relies on each member to perform their best and support each other, the church relies on its members to contribute their unique gifts and support the collective mission.

In both baseball and the Christian life, the principles of building relationships, fostering unity, and working together towards common goals are essential. For a baseball team, good team chemistry leads to better coordination, more efficient practices, and a positive and supportive team environment. For the church, strong relationships and unity lead to a more vibrant and effective community that can better fulfill its mission and support its members. By focusing on building good relationships and understanding team dynamics, whether on the baseball field or in the church, you can contribute to a more positive and successful environment. This requires effort, communication, trust, and a commitment to supporting and understanding each other. In both contexts, the benefits of building strong relationships and fostering unity are significant, leading to greater success, fulfillment, and a more positive experience for all involved.

In conclusion, building team chemistry is essential for a successful baseball team, just as building strong relationships with fellow believers and fostering unity in the church is crucial for a thriving Christian community. Both require a commitment to getting to know each other, effective communication, trust, and support. By working together and supporting each other, whether on the field or in the church, you can create a positive and effective environment that leads to success and fulfillment. The principles of building relationships, fostering unity, and working towards common goals are key to excelling in both areas, helping you to reach your full potential and contribute positively to your team and community. Whether playing baseball or participating in church activities, focusing on these principles will lead to a more successful and fulfilling experience.

Chapter 19 - Learn to Handle Pressure

"Be careful for nothing; but in every thing by prayer and supplication with thanksgiving let your requests be made known unto God." Philippians 4:6

To become a successful baseball player, learning to handle pressure is crucial. High-pressure situations can occur frequently in baseball, whether it's a crucial game-winning moment, a challenging pitch to a tough batter, or simply the overall stress of performing well for your team. Developing techniques to stay calm and focused during these moments can significantly enhance your performance. One effective technique is practicing deep breathing exercises, which help to calm your mind and reduce anxiety. By taking slow, deep breaths, you can lower your heart rate and clear your mind, making it easier to concentrate on the task at hand. Visualization is another powerful tool. By mentally rehearsing successful plays and positive outcomes, you can build confidence and prepare yourself for high-pressure situations. This involves imagining yourself executing perfect pitches, hitting crucial home runs, or making key defensive plays. Regularly practicing under simulated pressure can also help. Coaches can create practice scenarios that mimic the intensity of real-game situations, allowing players to become accustomed to the pressure and learn how to manage it effectively. Maintaining a positive mindset is essential as well. Focusing on your strengths, staying optimistic, and reminding yourself of past successes can boost your confidence and help you stay focused. Additionally, having a pre-game routine can provide a sense of stability and control, helping you to stay grounded and prepared.

In the life of a Christian, trusting in God and remaining steadfast in faith during challenging times is equally important. The Bible verse Philippians 4:6 says, "Be careful for nothing; but in every thing by prayer and supplication with thanksgiving let your requests be made known unto God." This verse encourages believers to trust in God and not be anxious about anything, but instead, to bring their concerns to God in prayer. Just as handling pressure is crucial for a baseball player, maintaining faith and trust in God during difficult times is essential for Christians. Prayer is a powerful way to manage stress and pressure. By bringing your worries and concerns to God, you can find peace and comfort knowing that He is in control. Prayer allows you to express your fears, seek guidance, and receive the reassurance that God is with you.

Developing a habit of regular prayer and supplication, combined with thanksgiving, helps to build a strong foundation of faith. By consistently turning to God in prayer, you cultivate a sense of reliance on Him, which can provide strength and stability during challenging times. Thanksgiving is an important aspect of this practice. By focusing on the blessings and expressing gratitude, you can shift your perspective from fear and anxiety to trust and contentment. Reflecting on past experiences where God has helped you through difficult situations can also strengthen your faith. Just as a baseball player remembers their successful moments to build confidence, Christians can recall times when God's guidance and support were evident in their lives.

Trusting in God involves letting go of the need to control every aspect of your life and believing that God has a plan and purpose for you. This can be particularly challenging during times of uncertainty or hardship, but it is during these times that faith is most important. Remaining steadfast in faith means holding onto your beliefs and trusting that God is working for your good, even when circumstances are difficult. Fellowship with other believers can provide additional support and encouragement. Sharing your struggles and victories with a faith community can offer comfort, advice, and prayer support, helping you to stay strong in your faith.

In both baseball and the Christian life, the ability to handle pressure effectively is a vital skill. For baseball players, staying calm and focused under pressure can lead to better performance and greater success on the field. For Christians, trusting in God and remaining steadfast in faith during challenging times can lead to spiritual growth and a deeper relationship with God. Both require a commitment to developing techniques and habits that help manage stress and maintain focus. By practicing these skills, whether on the baseball field or in your spiritual journey, you can build resilience, confidence, and strength.

In conclusion, learning to handle pressure is essential for a successful baseball player, just as trusting in God and remaining steadfast in faith during challenging times is crucial for a strong Christian life. Both require developing techniques to stay calm and focused, whether through deep breathing, visualization, prayer, or fellowship. By cultivating these habits, you can enhance your performance and maintain peace and trust during difficult times. The principles of managing pressure, staying focused, and relying on God are key to excelling in both areas, helping you to reach your full potential and live a fulfilling and impactful life. Whether facing high-pressure moments on the baseball field or navigating challenging times in your spiritual journey, these skills and practices can help you stay strong, confident, and steadfast.

Chapter 20 - Stay Positive

"Rejoice in the Lord always: and again I say, Rejoice." Philippians 4:4

Maintaining a positive attitude is crucial for success as a baseball player, especially in the face of setbacks and failures. Baseball, like many sports, involves a lot of ups and downs. There will be games where you hit a home run and games where you strike out multiple times. There will be moments when you make a game-winning catch and times when you miss an important play. The key to handling these fluctuations is to stay positive and keep a hopeful outlook. When you maintain a positive attitude, you are better equipped to handle failures and learn from them. Instead of dwelling on mistakes, you can focus on what you can do better next time. This mindset helps you to stay motivated and keep working hard, even when things don't go as planned. For example, if you have a bad game, instead of feeling defeated, you can analyze what went wrong and use it as an opportunity to improve. Positive thinking can also boost your confidence, which is essential for performing well under pressure. Believing in your abilities and staying optimistic about your potential can help you to stay calm and focused during challenging situations. Furthermore, a positive attitude can be contagious, lifting the spirits of your teammates and creating a supportive and encouraging team environment. When everyone on the team maintains a positive outlook, it can lead to better teamwork, communication, and overall performance. Celebrating small victories and acknowledging progress, no matter how minor, can also help to build and sustain a positive attitude.

In the life of a Christian, keeping a hopeful and positive outlook is equally important. The Bible verse Philippians 4:4 says, "Rejoice in the Lord always: and again I say, Rejoice." This verse encourages believers to maintain joy and positivity, trusting in God's plan regardless of circumstances. Just as maintaining a positive attitude is crucial for a baseball player, keeping a hopeful and positive outlook is essential for a Christian. Life is full of challenges, setbacks, and disappointments, but trusting in God's plan and remaining positive can help you navigate these difficulties with grace and resilience. When faced with challenges, instead of becoming discouraged, you can choose to focus on the positive aspects and trust that God has a purpose for everything that happens. This hopeful outlook is rooted in the belief that God is in control and that He works all things for the good of those who love Him. Maintaining a positive attitude as a Christian also involves rejoicing in the Lord and finding joy in His presence. This joy is not dependent on external circumstances but is a deep, abiding sense of happiness and peace that comes from knowing and trusting God. Regular prayer, reading the Bible, and worship can help to cultivate this joy and keep your focus on God's goodness and faithfulness.

A positive outlook can also help you to be more resilient in the face of trials. When you trust that God has a plan and that He is with you through every challenge, you can face difficulties with confidence and hope. This resilience is essential for maintaining your faith and continuing to grow spiritually, even when times are tough. Additionally, a positive attitude can inspire and uplift others. Just as a positive mindset can lift the spirits of your teammates, your hopeful and positive outlook can encourage and support those around you. Sharing your faith and your positive perspective can be a source of strength and inspiration for others, helping them to see the goodness of God and find hope in their own lives.

In both baseball and the Christian life, maintaining a positive attitude requires intentional effort and practice. It's easy to get discouraged by setbacks and failures, but by choosing to stay positive and hopeful, you can overcome these challenges and continue to move forward. This involves shifting your focus from what went wrong to what you can learn and how you can improve. It also involves surrounding yourself with supportive people who encourage and uplift you. In baseball, this might mean leaning on your coaches and teammates, while in the Christian life, it means seeking fellowship with other believers who can provide encouragement and support.

In conclusion, staying positive is essential for success as a baseball player, just as keeping a hopeful and positive outlook is crucial for a strong Christian life. Both require a commitment to focusing on the positives, learning from setbacks, and trusting in a greater plan. By maintaining a positive attitude, athletes can improve their performance, boost their confidence, and create a supportive team environment. Similarly, by keeping a hopeful outlook and trusting in God, Christians can navigate challenges with resilience, find joy in the Lord, and inspire others. The principles of positivity, hope, and trust are key to excelling in both areas, helping you to reach your full potential and live a fulfilling and impactful life. Whether on the baseball field or in your spiritual journey, maintaining a positive attitude allows you to face challenges with strength, confidence, and a joyful heart.

Chapter 21 - Injury Prevention

"Watch ye, stand fast in the faith, quit you like men, be strong." - 1 Corinthians 16:13

To become a successful baseball player, injury prevention is essential, and this involves learning and applying techniques to keep your body safe and strong. Proper warm-up routines and stretching are crucial components of injury prevention. Before any practice or game, it's important to warm up your muscles to increase blood flow and flexibility, which helps to reduce the risk of strains and sprains. A good warm-up can include light jogging, dynamic stretches, and sport-specific drills that gradually increase in intensity. Stretching helps to improve flexibility and range of motion, making it easier to perform various movements on the field. Static stretching, which involves holding a stretch for a period of time, is best done after a workout or game to help muscles recover and maintain flexibility. Additionally, strengthening exercises are vital for injury prevention. Building strong muscles, particularly in the core, legs, and arms, can support joints and improve overall stability. Regular strength training should focus on all major muscle groups to ensure balanced muscle development. Proper technique is also critical in preventing injuries. This means using the correct form when batting, pitching, fielding, and running to avoid putting unnecessary strain on your body. Coaches can provide guidance on proper techniques and help correct any bad habits that might lead to injury. It's also important to listen to your body and not push through pain, as this can lead to more serious injuries. Rest and recovery are key aspects of injury prevention as well. Ensuring you get enough rest between practices and games allows your body to repair and strengthen, reducing the risk of overuse injuries. Ice baths, massages, and adequate sleep can also aid in recovery. Wearing the right gear, such as properly fitted cleats and protective equipment, can provide additional support and protection. By consistently applying these techniques, you can reduce the risk of injury and maintain peak performance on the field. \In the life of a Christian, guarding your spiritual health by avoiding temptations and staying close to God is equally important. The Bible verse 1 Corinthians 16:13 says, "Watch ye, stand fast in the faith, quit you like men, be strong." This verse emphasizes the need to be vigilant, steadfast, and strong in faith. Just as injury prevention is crucial for a baseball player, maintaining spiritual health is vital for a Christian. Avoiding temptations involves being aware of the things that can lead you away from God and making conscious efforts to stay clear of them. This might include avoiding certain environments, people, or activities that encourage sinful behavior. It also means being mindful of your thoughts and actions, ensuring that they align with your faith and values.

Staying close to God is another important aspect of maintaining spiritual health. This involves regular prayer, reading the Bible, and participating in worship and fellowship with other believers. Prayer allows you to communicate with God, seek His guidance, and draw strength from His presence. Reading the Bible provides wisdom, encouragement, and a deeper understanding of God's will. Worship and fellowship help to keep your focus on God and provide a supportive community of fellow believers who can offer encouragement and accountability.

Just as proper warm-up and stretching routines prepare a baseball player's body for physical activity, spiritual disciplines prepare your soul for the challenges of life. By establishing a routine of prayer, Bible study, and worship, you can build a strong foundation of faith that helps you to stand firm in the face of temptation and difficulty. It's also important to surround yourself with a supportive community, much like a baseball team relies on each other for support and encouragement. Fellow believers can provide accountability, share wisdom, and help you stay on track in your spiritual journey.

In addition to these practices, it's important to strengthen your spiritual "muscles" through continuous learning and growth. This might involve attending Bible studies, reading Christian books, and seeking mentorship from more mature believers. By continually strengthening your faith, you can better withstand the pressures and temptations that come your way. Just as listening to your body is important for preventing physical injuries, listening to your conscience and the Holy Spirit is important for maintaining spiritual health. When you feel convicted about something, it's important to address it and seek forgiveness and guidance from God.

In conclusion, injury prevention is essential for maintaining peak performance as a baseball player, just as guarding your spiritual health by avoiding temptations and staying close to God is crucial for a strong Christian life. Both require a commitment to regular, proactive practices that keep you safe and strong. By learning and applying techniques to prevent injuries, such as proper warm-up routines and stretching, athletes can reduce the risk of injury and enhance their performance. Similarly, by staying vigilant, standing firm in the faith, and seeking God's guidance, Christians can maintain spiritual health and resilience. The principles of preparation, awareness, and proactive care are key to excelling in both areas, helping you to reach your full potential and live a fulfilling and impactful life. Whether on the baseball field or in your spiritual journey, taking steps to prevent harm and strengthen yourself can lead to greater success and well-being.

Chapter 22 - Adaptability

"To the weak became I as weak, that I might gain the weak: I am made all things to all men, that I might by all means save some." 1 Corinthians 9:22

To become a successful baseball player, adaptability is crucial. This means being open to learning new techniques and strategies, and being able to adjust to different situations on the field. Baseball is a dynamic game where conditions can change rapidly, and the ability to adapt can be the difference between success and failure. Whether it's adjusting your swing to hit different types of pitches, learning new fielding techniques to improve your defense, or changing your approach to base running depending on the situation, being adaptable helps you stay competitive and effective. Coaches often introduce new strategies and plays, and being open to these changes and willing to practice them diligently can make you a more versatile and valuable player. It's also important to learn from others, including teammates and opponents, who may have different approaches or techniques that can enhance your own game. Embracing change rather than resisting it allows you to continually improve and stay ahead of the competition. Adaptability also involves mental flexibility, such as staying calm under pressure, rebounding from mistakes quickly, and maintaining focus despite distractions or setbacks. By developing the ability to adapt, you can handle the unpredictable nature of the game and seize opportunities as they arise.

In the life of a Christian, being flexible and open to God's leading in different circumstances is equally important. The Bible verse 1 Corinthians 9:22 says, "To the weak became I as weak, that I might gain the weak: I am made all things to all men, that I might by all means save some." This verse highlights the importance of adaptability in reaching and serving others. Just as adaptability is crucial for a baseball player, being flexible and responsive to God's guidance is essential for a Christian. Life often presents unexpected challenges and opportunities, and being willing to adjust your plans and approach in response to God's leading can help you navigate these situations with faith and purpose.

Being adaptable in your faith means being open to new ways of serving God and others. This might involve stepping out of your comfort zone to take on new responsibilities in your church, adjusting your routines to make time for prayer and Bible study, or being willing to change your plans when you sense God is leading you in a different direction. It also means being open to learning and growing in your faith, whether through studying the Bible, participating in church activities, or seeking mentorship from more experienced believers. Just as a baseball player must continually refine their skills and learn new strategies, Christians must continually seek to grow in their understanding of God's Word and their ability to live it out.

Adaptability in faith also involves being sensitive to the needs and perspectives of others. Just as Paul was willing to adjust his approach to reach different people with the gospel, Christians are called to be flexible in how they interact with others, showing empathy and understanding. This can involve being willing to listen, adjusting your communication style, or finding creative ways to serve and support those around you. By being adaptable, you can more effectively share God's love and make a positive impact in the lives of others.

Additionally, being open to God's leading means trusting that He has a plan, even when things don't go as you expected. This trust allows you to remain flexible and responsive to His guidance, rather than being rigid or resistant to change. Just as a baseball player needs to stay focused and positive despite setbacks, Christians need to remain hopeful and trusting in God's plan, even when faced with challenges or uncertainties. This trust in God's sovereignty and goodness helps you to navigate life's twists and turns with faith and confidence. In both baseball and the Christian life, adaptability is key to success and growth. For baseball players, being adaptable allows you to continually improve, handle different game situations effectively, and stay competitive. For Christians, being adaptable helps you to respond to God's leading, serve others more effectively, and grow in your faith. Both require a willingness to learn, an openness to change, and a trust in the process. By cultivating adaptability, whether on the baseball field or in your spiritual journey, you can better handle challenges, seize opportunities, and achieve your goals.

In conclusion, adaptability is essential for becoming a successful baseball player, just as being flexible and open to God's leading is crucial for a strong Christian life. Both require a commitment to learning, a willingness to change, and a trust in a greater plan. By being adaptable, athletes can improve their skills, respond effectively to different game situations, and stay competitive. Similarly, by being open to God's leading and adaptable in how you serve and interact with others, Christians can grow in their faith, effectively share God's love, and make a positive impact in their communities. The principles of adaptability, openness, and trust are key to excelling in both areas, helping you to reach your full potential and live a fulfilling and impactful life. Whether on the baseball field or in your spiritual journey, being adaptable allows you to face challenges with confidence, embrace opportunities with enthusiasm, and navigate changes with grace and faith.

Chapter 23 - Good Sportsmanship

"And as ye would that men should do to you, do ye also to them likewise." Luke 6:31

To become a successful baseball player, demonstrating good sportsmanship is essential. Good sportsmanship means showing respect for your opponents, officials, and the game itself. Respecting your opponents means acknowledging their skills and efforts, even when the competition is intense. This can involve congratulating them on a good play, shaking hands after the game, and avoiding trash talk or negative comments. Respecting officials is equally important, as they are there to ensure the game is played fairly and safely. Even if you disagree with a call, responding respectfully and calmly is crucial. It shows maturity and helps maintain a positive atmosphere. Good sportsmanship also means playing by the rules and giving your best effort, whether you're winning or losing. When you play fair, you honor the game and all those who participate in it. If you make a mistake, such as committing a foul or error, owning up to it and striving to improve shows integrity. Celebrating your victories with humility and handling defeats with grace is another key aspect of sportsmanship. This means not gloating when you win and not making excuses when you lose. Instead, focus on what you learned and how you can improve. Encouraging and supporting your teammates, offering a positive attitude, and working together as a cohesive unit contribute to good team chemistry and a supportive environment. This spirit of camaraderie and mutual respect enhances the enjoyment and success of the team as a whole. Additionally, recognizing and appreciating the efforts of coaches, volunteers, and fans who support the game is part of good sportsmanship. They all contribute to the experience, and their efforts should be acknowledged and valued. Good sportsmanship fosters a positive environment where everyone can enjoy the game, learn, and grow.

In the life of a Christian, treating others with respect and kindness, demonstrating Christ's love, is equally important. The Bible verse Luke 6:31 says, "And as ye would that men should do to you, do ye also to them likewise." This verse, often referred to as the Golden Rule, encourages believers to treat others as they would like to be treated. Just as good sportsmanship is crucial for a baseball player, showing respect and kindness is essential for a Christian. This means treating everyone with dignity, compassion, and fairness, regardless of their background or circumstances. Demonstrating Christ's love involves being patient, forgiving, and generous in your interactions with others. It means going out of your way to help those in need, offering a kind word or gesture, and being a source of comfort and support.

Respecting others includes listening to their perspectives, valuing their contributions, and acknowledging their worth. This respect fosters a sense of community and mutual appreciation, whether in your church, neighborhood, or workplace. It also involves being mindful of how your actions and words affect others, striving to build up rather than tear down. Kindness is a powerful way to demonstrate Christ's love. Simple acts of kindness, such as offering a helping hand, sharing a smile, or speaking encouraging words, can make a significant impact on someone's day. These acts reflect the love and compassion that Jesus showed to others and help to spread positivity and goodwill.

Forgiveness is another important aspect of treating others with respect and kindness. Holding onto grudges and resentment can harm relationships and hinder personal growth. By forgiving others, you release the burden of anger and bitterness, paving the way for healing and reconciliation. This forgiveness reflects the grace that God extends to us and allows us to live in harmony with others. Additionally, generosity is a key component of demonstrating Christ's love. This can involve giving your time, resources, or talents to help others. Whether through volunteering, supporting charitable causes, or simply being there for someone in need, generosity shows a selfless commitment to the well-being of others.

In both baseball and the Christian life, the principles of respect, kindness, and integrity are fundamental. For baseball players, good sportsmanship enhances the experience for everyone involved, promoting a positive and respectful environment. For Christians, treating others with respect and kindness reflects the teachings of Jesus and helps to build strong, supportive communities. Both require a commitment to treating others with dignity, fairness, and compassion. By demonstrating these qualities, whether on the baseball field or in everyday life, you can make a positive impact and contribute to a better world.

In conclusion, good sportsmanship is essential for becoming a successful baseball player, just as treating others with respect and kindness is crucial for a strong Christian life. Both require a commitment to fairness, integrity, and compassion. By showing respect for opponents, officials, and the game itself, athletes can promote a positive and respectful environment. Similarly, by treating others with respect and kindness, Christians can demonstrate Christ's love and build supportive, compassionate communities. The principles of respect, kindness, and integrity are key to excelling in both areas, helping you to reach your full potential and live a fulfilling and impactful life. Whether on the baseball field or in your spiritual journey, practicing good sportsmanship and demonstrating Christ's love allows you to face challenges with grace, embrace opportunities with humility, and navigate life with a positive and respectful attitude.

Chapter 24 – Communication

"Let your speech be alway with grace, seasoned with salt, that ye may know how ye ought to answer every man." - Colossians 4:6

To become a successful baseball player, developing good communication skills is crucial for effectively interacting with coaches and teammates. Communication is the foundation of teamwork and understanding on and off the field. Good communication ensures that everyone is on the same page, whether it's calling out plays, signaling strategies, or offering encouragement. Clear and concise communication helps to avoid misunderstandings and mistakes that can lead to errors during the game. For example, when fielding a ball, players need to communicate who will catch it to avoid collisions. When batting, players need to understand the signals from the coach for bunts, steals, or hit-and-run plays. Effective communication with coaches is also essential for receiving and implementing feedback on performance. Coaches provide valuable insights and instructions to help players improve their skills and understand the game better. By actively listening and asking questions, players can clarify any doubts and ensure they are executing strategies correctly. Additionally, communicating openly with teammates fosters a sense of camaraderie and trust. Encouraging words, constructive criticism, and positive reinforcement contribute to a supportive team environment where everyone feels valued and motivated to perform their best. Developing good communication skills involves practicing active listening, speaking clearly, and being respectful and considerate in all interactions. This helps to build strong relationships and ensures smooth coordination during games and practices.

In the life of a Christian, effective and loving communication is equally important within the body of Christ. The Bible verse Colossians 4:6 says, "Let your speech be alway with grace, seasoned with salt, that ye may know how ye ought to answer every man." This verse emphasizes the importance of speaking with grace and wisdom. Just as communication is vital for a baseball player, it is essential for Christians to communicate effectively and lovingly with others. This means expressing thoughts and feelings clearly while being mindful of the impact of your words. Speaking with grace involves being kind, gentle, and respectful, even in difficult conversations. It means choosing words that uplift and encourage rather than tear down. Being "seasoned with salt" implies adding wisdom and thoughtfulness to your speech, ensuring that your words are both truthful and beneficial to the listener.

Effective communication within the body of Christ helps to build unity, resolve conflicts, and strengthen relationships. It allows for open and honest dialogue, where members can share their joys, struggles, and needs. By listening actively and empathetically, Christians can provide support and understanding to one another. This fosters a sense of community and belonging, where everyone feels heard and valued. Communication is also key in teaching and sharing the gospel. By articulating the message of Christ clearly and lovingly, Christians can reach out to others and spread the good news effectively. This requires not only knowledge of the Bible but also the ability to connect with people and address their questions and concerns thoughtfully.

In both baseball and the Christian life, the principles of effective communication, respect, and active listening are fundamental. For baseball players, good communication enhances teamwork, coordination, and performance. For Christians, effective and loving communication builds a strong, supportive community and helps to share the message of Christ. Both require a commitment to developing these skills and using them thoughtfully and respectfully. By focusing on clear, kind, and wise communication, whether on the baseball field or within the body of Christ, you can foster better relationships, enhance teamwork, and create a positive and encouraging environment. In conclusion, developing good communication skills is essential for becoming a successful baseball player, just as communicating effectively and lovingly is crucial for a strong Christian life. Both require a commitment to clarity, respect, and kindness in all interactions. By communicating effectively with coaches and teammates, athletes can ensure better coordination, teamwork, and performance. Similarly, by speaking with grace and wisdom, Christians can build strong, supportive communities and effectively share the message of Christ. The principles of clear communication, active listening, and respect are key to excelling in both areas, helping you to reach your full potential and live a fulfilling and impactful life. Whether on the baseball field or in your spiritual journey, practicing good communication allows you to connect with others, navigate challenges with understanding, and create a positive and supportive environment.

Chapter 25 - Love for the Game

"Thou shalt love the Lord thy God with all thy heart, and with all thy soul, and with all thy mind." Matthew 22:37

To become a successful baseball player, developing good communication skills and cultivating a genuine love for the game are crucial. Good communication skills are essential for effectively interacting with coaches and teammates, ensuring that everyone understands their roles and responsibilities on the field. Clear and concise communication helps prevent misunderstandings and mistakes, which can lead to better coordination and performance. For instance, players need to call out plays, signal strategies, and offer encouragement to one another during a game. Effective communication with coaches is also important for receiving and implementing feedback on your performance. Coaches provide valuable insights and instructions to help you improve your skills and understand the game better. By actively listening and asking questions, you can clarify any doubts and ensure you are executing strategies correctly. Communicating openly with teammates fosters a sense of camaraderie and trust, contributing to a supportive team environment where everyone feels valued and motivated to perform their best. Developing good communication skills involves practicing active listening, speaking clearly, and being respectful and considerate in all interactions. This helps build strong relationships and ensures smooth coordination during games and practices.

In addition to communication, cultivating a genuine love for baseball is essential for driving your commitment and enjoyment of the sport. When you have a deep passion for the game, you are more likely to stay motivated and dedicated, even during challenging times. Loving the game means enjoying every aspect of it, from practicing and improving your skills to competing and being part of a team. This passion fuels your desire to work hard, overcome obstacles, and continually strive for excellence. It also makes the experience more enjoyable, allowing you to have fun and appreciate the sport, regardless of the outcome of each game. To cultivate a love for the game, immerse yourself in all its aspects: watch professional games, learn about its history, and practice regularly. Engage with other players and fans who share your enthusiasm, and celebrate both your achievements and those of your teammates. A genuine passion for baseball can make the hard work and sacrifices feel worthwhile, driving your commitment and enhancing your overall experience.

In the life of a Christian, developing a deep love for God and His Word is equally important. The Bible verse Matthew 22:37 says, "Thou shalt love the Lord thy God with all thy heart, and with all thy soul, and with all thy mind." This verse emphasizes the importance of loving God completely, which fuels your commitment to the faith. Just as a love for baseball drives your dedication to the sport, a deep love for God and His Word drives your commitment to living out your faith. This love motivates you to spend time in prayer, study the Bible, and participate in worship and fellowship with other believers. It helps you to stay faithful and persevere through challenges, knowing that your relationship with God is the most important aspect of your life. Developing a deep love for God involves regularly engaging with His Word, reflecting on His goodness, and seeking to understand His will for your life. It also means showing love and kindness to others, as an expression of your love for God.

In both baseball and the Christian life, the principles of good communication and genuine passion are fundamental. For baseball players, effective communication and a love for the game enhance teamwork, coordination, and performance. For Christians, loving God and His Word deeply strengthens your faith and commitment to living out His teachings. Both require a commitment to practicing these principles consistently and wholeheartedly. By focusing on clear, respectful communication and cultivating a genuine passion, whether for baseball or your faith, you can achieve greater success and fulfillment.

In conclusion, developing good communication skills and cultivating a love for the game are essential for becoming a successful baseball player, just as communicating effectively and developing a deep love for God and His Word are crucial for a strong Christian life. Both require a commitment to clarity, respect, and passion in all interactions. By communicating effectively with coaches and teammates, athletes can ensure better coordination, teamwork, and performance. Similarly, by loving God with all your heart, soul, and mind, Christians can deepen their faith, fuel their commitment, and live out their beliefs more fully. The principles of clear communication, active listening, and genuine passion are key to excelling in both areas, helping you to reach your full potential and live a fulfilling and impactful life. Whether on the baseball field or in your spiritual journey, practicing good communication and cultivating a deep love for what you do allows you to connect with others, navigate challenges with understanding, and create a positive and supportive environment.

Following these steps will help you become a more skilled and successful baseball player, allowing you to enjoy the game and perform at your best. Similarly, applying these principles in your spiritual life will help you grow in faith, live out your beliefs effectively, and deepen your relationship with God.

Don't miss out!

Visit the website below and you can sign up to receive emails whenever Joshua Rhoades publishes a new book. There's no charge and no obligation.

https://books2read.com/r/B-A-AJLBB-HTHWE

BOOKS 2 READ

Connecting independent readers to independent writers.

Did you love *From Dugout to Devotion- Spiritual Lessons from Baseball*? Then you should read *Driven By Faith: Motor Racing Inspired Christian Life*[1] by Joshua Rhoades!

[2]

"Driven By Faith - Motor Racing Inspired Christian Life" is a captivating fusion of high-speed motor racing and the profound journey of Christian faith. This book accelerates readers into the thrilling world of car racing, drawing powerful parallels between the intricacies of the track and the daily walk of a Christian.Each chapter is meticulously crafted to offer practical Scriptural applications, drawing from the wisdom of the Bible to illuminate the principles of motor racing. Readers will explore how the discipline of maintaining a race car mirrors the spiritual maintenance needed in a Christian's life, with Scriptures highlighting the importance of regular prayer, study, and fellowship.The book considers

---

1. https://books2read.com/u/mlGrP9

2. https://books2read.com/u/mlGrP9

the technicalities of racing, from the precision of pit stops to the strategy of overtaking, illustrating how these elements reflect the Christian virtues of patience, perseverance, and trust in God's timing. Passages like Hebrews 12:1-2 and others, come alive as readers see the race set before them, encouraged to run with endurance and keep their eyes on Jesus, the ultimate champion of faith."Driven By Faith" is rich with detailed insights into the world of motor racing, from the adrenaline of the starting grid to the triumph of the checkered flag. Yet, it is equally rich in spiritual depth, offering readers a roadmap for navigating the twists and turns of life with grace and faith.Whether you're a motorsport enthusiast, a devout Christian, "Driven By Faith - Motor Racing Inspired Christian Life" will fuel your spirit and inspire your soul. Prepare to embark on a journey where faith and racing unite, driving you toward the ultimate finish line with victory in Christ.